Heal. Peel. Grow.

One Girl's Journey, from Breaking Down to Waking up, and the Lessons Learned Along the Way

By Alexis Billings

To my Jake.
The greatest soul I've ever known.
I will forever be grateful for you.
I will love you always.

Heal. Peel. Grow. is a true testament to the transformation of the work. Alexis' own spiritual awakening and the lessons she embodied on the journey is a gift to the collective. If you are in the midst of your own journey, I highly suggest this book as the reader is taken through a unique, heart centered perspective.

- Dr. Nicole LePare, The Holistic Psychologist

Acknowledgements

Jake, you're my number one. Thank you for never giving up on me. Thank you for your trust in me and allowing me to be who I am down to my rawest layer.

My sister Talia, thank you for being there for me when I couldn't show up for myself. Thank you for your patience when it takes me a minute to hear your messages. Thank you for your time and energy with this book and for your support of my dreams. WUSM.

My Mom and Dad, you two are very special people. Thank you for your guidance, love, and for giving me a beautiful life. You've both always supported where I've wanted to go even if you didn't understand it. Thank you for that respect. I love you with all of my heart.

The established authors to whom I spoke with, for your help in guiding me through the "How-To" of publishing in support of this book coming to life: Sheryl Green, Rae Wilson and Paul Papa.

Clare, Lauren, Ronnie and Haily, thank you for being my beta readers. Thank you for the time you spent providing loving feedback. I am so grateful for your support and the time spent on this book.

Dr. Nicole LePare, thank you from the bottom of my heart for your words and support on my book. Your work is incredibly needed in this world. You are a gift in many ways and a mentor to me.

My editor, Taryn. You did a bang up job and I seriously needed you. Thank you!

My best friend Deonna, you have my roots. You are such a comfort and I love sharing our stories daily. Thank you for your unconditional support through this story and all of my stories since we met in middle school.

Preface

I began writing this book with the intention of keeping it to myself, as I was knee deep in my healing and transformational work at the time. It wasn't until a couple years later that I received a message to publish it for others to read. I had heard Gabby Berstein say, "When you transform spiritually, it becomes your responsibility to clear fear and share your truth with the world." Upon reflection, I wondered what kind of value I could share with others through my story? The lessons that lead to my spiritual transformation, of course. The things I found myself to be so passionate about while writing this. Lessons that helped make me better.

This is how we enrich our lives: by learning from our experiences and one another. I feel that this is the beauty in sharing our stories - sharing our pain. We all struggle, and my story is likely to be many people's story. Although it may seem so, we are not alone during these dark times. By sharing our truth and owning it together we can inspire each other to heal. This is a part of my journey that I think many will relate to. If I can share this with you and it helps, inspires, enlightens your world, provides comfort and connection during a confusing, lost time for you, then it will be well worth being vulnerable with people I may never meet.

So, this is for the soul searchers, the deep thinkers, the overly sensitives, the self-helpers, the self-developers, the self-healers, the seekers, and creators of the world. I share this for you.

Moving to Nevada

April 15th – April 21st 2012

The excitement had tingled throughout my whole body for weeks now, getting more intense as the day drew near. We were finally doing it! Moving across the country to follow our dreams. To top it all off, we were driving there! To say I felt excited was an understatement; I was elated. I was about to go on my greatest adventure yet, and start over with the love of my life.

We called it a "lifestyle move." Vegas offered the perfect combination of a warm, dry climate, incredible scenery, plenty of outdoor adventure, and low-cost living. We thought, Vegas is going to be the perfect place to live. Through the freshly cleaned windshield, surrounded by gray sky and lush green trees, I stared ahead at my future, filled with dreams and uncertainty.

* * *

It was as if we were airdropped from a helicopter, landing in unfamiliar territory. We're down on all fours, several feet apart, looking up at each other. My blonde hair tangling in the wind as it blows wildly around my face. The desert dust swirling in the air, clouding my vision; I'm barely able to see Jake, let alone hear him, as the noise surrounding us fills my ears. The desert sun beats down on us. We squint into each others eyes while chaos dances around us and we decide to run.

The desert heat scorching, the dust settling, we are surrounded by open freedom.

We're moving so fast we can't even take notice of what's around us. I begin to lose sight of Jake, no longer able to tell the distance between us. Is he next to me? Are we even on the same path anymore? I can see his body moving in the distance but cannot call out. The direction I'm heading in is unclear.

My whole body is being pulled forward, and no matter how hard I try to dig my heels into the dirt, I can't stop.

I no longer have any idea where I am. I'm surrounded by trees; but the last time I looked, I was in a desert. Now, green lush bushes and, full, thick trees surround me. For the first time in I don't know how long, I've slowed. There is little light where I am and my voice still isn't working.

My body cannot fight this force still pulling me forward. My mind isn't telling me to stop or turn around, so I keep moving. Curiosity fuels me. I'm not happy or sad. I'm not scared, worried or excited. I'm numb. I move forward.

My pace picks up and I am racing again. How can I be moving so quickly? Thoughts do not last long here. They leave my head as fast as they enter. I can't hold on to any ideas. Clarity is not with me. All I can do is move forward.

And there it is, at last. A light. A view. An opening. I can see the trees part ahead and there is a clearing. I can see mountains, blue skies and white, puffy clouds. I can see clearly. With desperation fueling me, I pick up the pace and run to the clearing. I'm almost there and with my last step, I drop.

My breath leaves my body. The drop is long but fast. Looking up at the cliff I just ran off of, it's getting farther and farther away, which only means one thing...

I guess when you fall that hard from a place that high, breaking is the only option.

Breaking hurts.

...Suddenly, I could feel again.

As I lay there looking up at where I just was, the realization of what I had done hit me.

* * *

Part 1: The Affair

September 2012 – September 2013

My phone buzzed with an alert of a text message, as it had done on a daily basis since July. My heart fluttered in anticipation as I walked over to my phone.

"Hey, Lex!" It was Him. I knew Him so well I could hear the tone of his voice through text. "Hi!!"

And so it began, as it did every day for the past two months. Here I was, going about my day, trying to build a business as a fitness trainer, living in Henderson (a town outside of Las Vegas) with my boyfriend of seven years, and texting with a buddy from my youth.

It started off innocently, two old friends reconnecting over a common theme: starting over in new states to live more authentic lives.

My boyfriend, Jake, and I had just moved into our own apartment after living with my Dad for four months. Jake found a job pretty quickly. His days consisted of waking up at 3:30AM to be at work, then after work, he spent the majority of his time exploring the Vegas trails on his mountain bike.

I started my business within weeks of arriving, using Groupon to promote my boot-camp classes at a local park. I spent two days a week waking up at 6am to teach my morning class, returning again in the evenings at 7PM. Other days, I'd train clients at 5:30am and 9am, and come home to an empty house only to head out the door for another client at noon. I'd come home afterward, have lunch, and then plan routines for my next class or for my client sessions. Later in the afternoon, I'd head out to train another client, and on the two days a week that I taught class, I'd go straight to the park until 8pm.

Sounds like a busy, fulfilling day, right? Well, I was actually shying away from challenging myself and, because of that, I was lonely and bored. So I did what any emotionally and mentally unhealthy, fearful, insecure, unaware, 28 year old would do; I sought happiness outside of myself.

Seeking happiness outside of yourself is much easier than dealing with the actual problem you may be facing. Listening to that voice in our heads called the Ego, which steers you away from vulnerability and instills fear, doubt and anxiety in us, is far too scary.

Seeking happiness outside of myself kept me from focusing on growing my business, yet I was convinced that I was, in fact, very happy with my life. On the surface, I was living the life I had moved to Vegas to live: starting a business and teaching fitness classes. However, that is not the only thing I was doing on a daily basis and my business was not growing.

Looking back, I realize the text messages were providing instant gratification during a scary and lonely time in which, I was so afraid to stand in my truth and exhibit raw vulnerability that I had no idea what the fuck I was doing.

I was afraid to meet new people; I was from a small town and now lived in a large city. Small fish, big ocean. I was intimidated to put myself out there, and too insecure to step forward.

I was also tired of feeling like I needed help with everything I did. I spent my whole life feeling like that. I was the baby in the family and, due to a "slight learning disability" I had to repeat first grade, so I was helpless. At least, this is the message I was given. My mom didn't push me to do better or overcome challenges, instead she would literally say, "Lexie can't handle that." Therefore, I never developed the confidence or problem-solving skills to overcome difficulties on my own. Unaware that it was my self-limiting belief, I spent thirty-something years carrying that story.

You might be thinking, "It's not your mom's fault; you're an adult, stop blaming her." We'll get to that later. At the time, that is where I was: no confidence in my capabilities and a lack of awareness of what they even were. And so, with an absence of understanding where true happiness and fulfillment came from, I decided to engage with Him because it felt really damn good.

In fact, it felt so good that I became intensely emotionally dependent on Him. So much so, that when He tried to back off in early September shortly after Jake and I moved into our apartment, I convinced Him that there was no need. Everything was fine and we weren't doing anything wrong. When He probed, "Does your boyfriend know we talk every day?" I replied simply, "He knows we talk. He's fine with it."

I stretched the truth for survival. That might sound a tad dramatic but it was truly how I felt. That day when He tried to back off and I did not receive a text from Him, I felt a suffocating dread roll over me. A desperation in my heart for the attention I craved from Him. A knot in the pit of my stomach fearing the end of our relationship. I couldn't fathom not speaking to Him daily, so I stretched the truth. Jake knew we spoke; he did not know we spoke daily.

At that point, the messages were still harmless. We would discuss movies, music, the past, working out, and what we'd done that day. We would toss compliments to each other and stroke each others egos.

It wasn't until November that I knew a line had been crossed, surprisingly by Him; but, I allowed it. He started calling me.

My phone rang one afternoon while I was planning for my next class. My heart sank to the pit of my stomach when I saw it was Him. I wasn't sure if I should feel excited, ashamed or nervous. I'd never been in such a situation before and I was torn between curiosity and discipline. I'm sure you can guess which one won...

"That was harmless," I thought as I hung up and tried to shrug it off.

But I couldn't. In the car later that afternoon driving to my next appointment, I struggled with a guilty high. An awareness that accepting the call was probably wrong. And unnecessary. And that if it happened again, I'd have to do something about it.

But it felt so good.

It did happen again. Shortly after Thanksgiving. And I did nothing. Instead, I allowed myself to feel the joy of His affection toward me because I was so incredibly empty inside.

I had hated Thanksgiving that year. I had hated being away from my Mom and from familiarity. I had hated going to my Dad's house, where he lived with his wife, who's the same age as me, and their two children. I had hated that I was with a guy who couldn't pull me out of my gloom and help me to focus on what I knew was important during the holidays: family. I couldn't see that I was lucky to have family around, even if it looked different than expected.

So I indulged in conversations with Him. We spoke about our Thanksgiving holiday and our plans to return to Connecticut for Christmas. We talked of the music and bands we were listening to. He had no desire to get off the phone but I was nervous. I was scared. I was racked with guilt. So I said I had to go.

Over the following days, He called again.
And again.
And again.

The next time He called, Jake was around, so I took it outside. I stood in the parking lot of our apartment complex, in the freezing December desert winter, shivering as we spoke about our trip "home" and possibly seeing each other. We spoke of how crazy it was that we had lost touch seven years ago and reconnected, only to become super-close friends. We talked and talked and talked and an hour later, when the conversation was done, I made my way back to my building.

As I walked, I remembered how thin the building walls were. We could always hear people outside talking at night. I knew it was possible that Jake had overheard some of my conversation. In fact, Jake would think it was odd, in and of itself, that I had taken a call outside in the middle of winter, a season that I loathe. I knew then that he had to have been listening. I thought fast.

"Who was that?" His face was serious when I entered the warmth of the apartment.

"It was my sister, at first. She's having some troubles," I lied. *I can't believe I fucking lied.* Then I confessed that He had called to talk about possibly getting together over Christmas. "I was just returning his call." *That's still a fucking lie.*

The second time He called when Jake was around, I couldn't lie again. I could've ignored the call but that didn't feel like an option either; I didn't want it to look like I was hiding something. So I took it. It was uncomfortable and I hated trying to hide my conversation from Jake while He joked about visiting me in Las Vegas. I was positive that, at this point, Jake was suspicious. He's not an idiot.

The third time He called when Jake was around I ignored it, but then decided to go for a "run" and call Him back. When He didn't answer, I felt panic and anxiety. My tummy had butterflies. I wanted to hear His voice. I *needed* to hear His voice. Our conversations had become almost like a necessity to my day. I continued to run a bit more before calling it quits and heading back to the apartment. Of course, that was when He called me back. I went outside again to take the call.

Why was I taking the call outside? What was I hiding if the conversations were, in fact, innocent?

I was hiding the tone of my voice. My smile. The genuine affection for Him that I was not supposed to be feeling.

When I came in from the cold, I asked Jake if it would be alright if I grabbed dinner with Him while in Connecticut over Christmas. Jake was not going to be making the trip back with me that year, as he had not earned the time off from work. He agreed that dinner seemed innocent enough. I smiled with relief.

* * *

Christmas
Our plan was for me to grab Him from the airport, stop at His mom's house, and then head over to a popular local restaurant in town. We also had planned for me to spend the night at His house. Yes, Jake knew about it and trusted me.

I rolled up to the airport and waited, periodically checking my rear view mirror for a figure that resembled Him. It had been almost a year since I'd seen Him. Before that, it had been seven. I was caught up in the moment, not focused on any ramifications.

I was excited to see Him. Though not for the reasons one might think after reading the past few pages. I was actually hoping that nothing about the past few months would come up tonight. I truly just loved being in His company. He is light-hearted. Funny. Easy to talk to. A nice guy. I wanted to enjoy our friendship like we had ten years ago.

Then, there He was: strolling out of the building in a gray hoodie, loose jeans and a baseball hat. I didn't feel butterflies, but the excitement stayed with me.

I jumped out of my mom's car, a smile ripped across my face as I walked toward Him. But his face... he had never looked at me like that before. Not even when we were teenagers. His smile touched his eyes. Those blue stones with a slight downward slant on the outer ends, gleamed at me.

His thick arms wrapped around me and lifted me up against his body. For the first time in months, I felt that familiarity I had been longing. As He placed me down, he grabbed my waist, exclaiming how skinny I was. I was the thinnest I'd been in my adult life at 5'10 and 119lbs (That's another part of the story that I'll get to later).

As we drove to his house, gushing enthusiastically over getting together, it was the first time in six months that I felt at home. My surroundings were familiar; I knew where I was. I felt the feelings that had been missing ever since moving: belonging and comfort.

Yet, if I had allowed myself to *really* think about what I was feeling —to *really* go deep— I actually felt terrified. Like I was in the middle of the dark, expansive ocean, treading water to keep from sinking. Completely alone, with nothing around me to grab hold of. There was no sign of a ship coming to save me, no sign of a buoy to cling to or land to swim to. I couldn't see what was beneath the surface. It was just me, in a dangerous situation that had huge potential threats to the life that I had built. If I had allowed myself to go that deep, I would have seen that I was terrified of where I was.

So, I never allowed myself to think that deeply.

Things went as planned. We arrived at His mom's house and I visited with His mom while He got ready. Though our conversations had been few, I had always loved His mom. When I looked into her eyes, I felt I could see her soul. That doesn't happen with everybody. Her light blue eyes revealed her raw vulnerability, pain, strength and love. She is a strong woman. I saw that in her and cherished it.

Once He was ready, we left for the restaurant. We found a table in the bar and ordered drinks. Our waitress was bubbly and engaging and the perfect audience for Him. He was charming, charismatic, funny, and disarming and He liked to show off a little bit. People smiled often when interacting with him and I think He enjoyed being the one who did that for them.

I played off of that personality well, too. I jumped in and told her how we were "old friends" but now lived in different states. She shared where she was from and that she attended Sacred Heart.

When she left, He looked at me and said, "See Lex, I love that about you. You can talk to anyone."

He was good at stroking my ego; the last six months had been full of comments like that. I didn't realize I was starved for it until He and I reconnected again. He was always quick to point out things about me He liked. Of course, with that came the opposite, pointing out things He didn't like about me. But that would come when we would fight and that comes later.

He asked about my life with Jake. How long have you been together? Seven years.
Did you want kids? No.
Was I happy? Yeah.

"If he asked you to marry him right now, what would you say?"

Hesitantly, I looked up at Him with half a smile, "What?" Confusion in my voice.

"If, when you got back to Vegas, he asked you to marry him—like the day you got back—what would you say?"

The waves in that deadly ocean began to pick up and I could see storm clouds rolling in.

No, no, no! Please don't go down this road.

I felt a pressure to answer quickly because what would it reveal if I hesitated for one more second? I said yes. Because I thought I should say yes. Because I never imagined, in all my time with Jake, how it could ever be a no. But, at that moment, it felt like a lie. Maybe there had been a slight uncertainty in my voice that He sensed because then he asked the question I had been dreading. He brought up the topic I had hoped to avoid. He asked calmly, with genuine curiosity and true gentleness, "Lex, isn't it crazy that we've been talking every single day for the last six months? I haven't talked to anyone else every day for the last six months."

He had a smile on his face. He was excited and happy that we had been talking so frequently.

I tried to stay relaxed, confident, not threatened. My arms folded on the table. "Yeah, I know." My voice timid and soft.

"I like it. I feel like it's like a movie; old friends reconnecting after seven years, living in different states..." He smiled.

"Yeah." I nodded with a smile, completely unsure of what else to say.

"I think about you every day. Like, what it would be like to be with you." He paused briefly. His voice quieted, "I'm starting to feel things for you, ya know? What about you, are you feeling anything?"

Fuck. Fuck. Fuck.

The dark clouds are directly overhead and it is pouring on me.

The balls. The nerve of this guy.

And yet, I didn't shut it down. In my head I was thinking, *Of course I'm feeling things! How could I not be? My relationship with you has flourished more in the last 6 months than the one I have with the guy I've been living with. I feel like I'm 17 again!*

"Yeah." I answered honestly, fidgeting with my beer in front of me.

"Do you ever wonder what it would be like to be together again?"

Shut it down. Shut it down. Shut it down. That's what I should have done. That's what a healthy, secure person would have done. But nope. Not me. I ached for the affection. The attention. Being desired. Being thought of daily.

"What do you mean? Like, live with you?" I asked.

"Yeah. I can see you there with me." He leaned in with a smile.

Oh my God. My heart sank. I felt so guilty, but it felt so good at the same time.

"Well, I don't really see how that would work, being that you want kids and I don't." I played.

Then he said something really beautiful. "Lex, having kids is about starting a family with someone you love."It probably wasn't that rare of a viewpoint, but I had never heard it said in such a way before.

"Lex, having kids is about starting a family with someone you love."

It probably sounds obvious to many, but I had never looked at having kids in that way.

When I was little, I thought having kids was something people did just because they were "supposed to". I remember as a teenager not really wanting kids, but not seeking another path for my life. I would sit in my room planning my life, mindlessly assigning the number of children I'd have by some random age that seemed reasonable. There were no conversations in my house about what I wanted to do when I was older. To be honest, there were never conversations about what I wanted, period.

Then, in college, I met Jake. This tall, incredibly soulful human being with stone dark eyes, and long brown curly hair that peeked out from under his baseball cap. We had an art class together. He was calm, confident, quiet, sensitive, and smart.

Jake had a different point of view regarding kids: you don't have to have kids just because the majority chooses to. It made me start to wonder about my motives for wanting children.

After college, I really began to think more deeply about his idea of not having kids, but I was unsure. I was going through a very dark, challenging time, as my family structure had been altered and the shift left me questioning many things.

My parents had divorced and, within five years, my father dated, got pregnant, and married a girl my exact age. I was 19 when they met and 24 when they got married and had their first baby. It was my father's fourth child from a third woman.

That was just months after I graduated college. What should have been a very blissful, carefree time, quickly morphed into a dark and angry time, as I lacked the skills and awareness to deal with such challenges in a healthy way.

At the time, I was completely turned off to the concept of family.

Then, that night at the restaurant in Connecticut, He dropped lines about having kids for the sole reason of creating more love by having a family with someone you love. It was a mental picture I felt distant from.

He challenged me with this other point of view. I was grateful for His remarks; they were refreshing and thought provoking. They also made me more drawn to Him than I already had been.

My head tilted to the side and my eyes narrowed as I stared at Him with my mouth open. "Uh, I've never heard it put that way before," I replied.

And so, the conversation went deeper. It went very deep. It went down a path that was quite dangerous. Together we explored what might be if I chose to take a risk. We played with the possibility of being together again. While I had hoped to avoid the topic, the conversation held me accountable for my actions over the previous months. It couldn't be ignored.

After dinner, there was a heaviness in me. A dread. I now needed to deal with our relationship, whatever it was, and I so did not want to. We pulled up to His house and, before we went in, He asked how I was doing and what I'd thought of our conversation. I had always appreciated how reflective He was, as it made Him very easy to talk to. Being that I'm also reflective, we eased into honest conversation.

I shrugged and told Him I needed to think about some things. There was silence.

And then He did it. He leaned in to kiss me. Everything about that night had felt so good. How He had walked out of the airport and wrapped his arms around me. His compliments. Our conversation. The familiarity and comfort of being in His company was so lovely. But not this. This was wrong on every level and I didn't want it. Not like this. Before our lips met, I turned my head and caught His forehead on mine with a sigh.

"I can't," I whispered. "I'm sorry. I just can't do that."

As if that would take away all the other things I shouldn't have done or felt in the last six months. But it didn't. And I knew it. I had made a huge mess.

"Okay." He replied softly, forgiving me.

We went inside.

It was implied that we would continue with the rest of the night as if nothing had just happened. We went to the basement, where I'd be sleeping, and popped in one of His favorite movies (always one of His favorites, never one of mine).

He left me to sleep around 1am.

In the morning, I woke with a knot in my stomach. The blissful reconnection was abruptly over. I had to face reality.

He had plans with His family that day and I needed to get my Mom's car back to her. I was going to miss Him.

He sat on the couch with me and asked, "So, what are you going to do?"

I shrugged.

He shared with me that his heart ached.

At that point, I was wondering if it was possible to be in love with two different people. I just loved that when I looked at Him I felt at home. Not that I hadn't ever felt those things with Jake, I had. But they got lost somewhere along the way and I hadn't even noticed they were gone. I thought we'd been living a great life, and then all of a sudden, we weren't.

I sat on the couch next to Him, looking at his kind face. The face that I had known since I was a teenager. He knew me, could figure me out and read me so easily. I loved the downward slant in his eyes and how easy it was to converse with Him. He confided and opened up to me easily. It wasn't like pulling teeth. He thought about things and shared them with me openly. We had a trust.

He wanted to know what I was going to do. I didn't want it to ever come to this. I never wanted it to reach this point but there it was, staring me in the face.

I looked down at my hands in my lap. I thought about my life with Jake. How much love we had. How long we'd been together and how I never thought I'd ever consider being with someone else. Then I looked up at Him. "I don't think I'm that kind of risk taker," I replied softly. I cringed at the thought of disappointing Him.

He took a deep breath but I think He knew it was coming. "Yeah." He nodded.

We had feelings for each other but we knew it was over. After breakfast, I showered and left.

He carried my bag out to my car and, with a heavy heart, we hugged. Oh, his hugs—he was never the first to let go. He always held on longer than I did. Since we were teenagers.

As I drove home, I cried. I cried so hard I thought I'd need to pull over. I couldn't believe the pain I was in. I just couldn't believe it. I hurt so badly. My body and my heart hurt so badly. I felt like I was going through an actual break up. Heck, maybe I was! To this day I'm not fully sure. I guess, maybe, it was like a breakup. We had spoken daily for six months and had feelings for each other...

I began to recall all the things we had gone through since we were teens. Replaying our story together as if I were trying to hold on to something or justify my pain over the story's ending.

My reaction scared me. I knew something deeper was going on, but I had no idea what it was. I called Him after I dropped off the car. I bought some time; I told Him that I wasn't quite sure what was going on and that I needed to think about it more. I was more distraught over our ending than He was; I could tell even then, but I ignored it.

At that point, I had found a buoy in the ocean. The ocean had calmed and the rain had stopped. I was safe on my buoy until the next shit storm arrived.

Then I called Jake.

Jake is not an idiot. Not in the slightest. I never suspected him to be. I told him I had some things on my mind and I wanted to talk when I got home. That must not have felt good for him to hear. Though, to be honest, I didn't even think about his feelings at the time. I was too focused on getting through the holiday, which I knew that was going to be hard.

God, would you listen to me? I had left my boyfriend of seven years alone in Las Vegas over Christmas because I was so caught up in my own stupid fucking shit.

* * *

I got home from my trip and everything was different between Jake and I; everything that had once been familiar now felt so foreign.

Three weeks after meeting Jake, I knew I would marry him. Seven years later, I was having an emotional affair. What the fuck happened? I wasn't sure. I truly did not understand how we got there, so I wasn't ready to admit to anything.

It was a torturous conversation. I lead with wanting kids. At the time, I thought possibly wanting kids had something to do with what had happened. But I can tell you now, it did not. It was heartbreaking to look at a man with the greatest soul I'd ever known and tell him, I think we need to separate. Jake is a man of few words, but with deep thoughts. Though he doesn't say much, he thinks deeply and is sensitive and has a soul truly unlike any other man I have ever met. There I was, tearing it apart.

Like I said, it was foreign. We had been on the road to marriage, so we didn't make any drastic decisions. We continued to have intense conversations. But again, Jake is not an idiot, he knew something was up.

Part 2: The Breakup

January 9th 2013

I no longer have any idea where I am. I'm surrounded by trees; but the last time I looked, I was in a desert. Now, green lush bushes and full, thick trees surround me. For the first time in I don't know how long, I've slowed. There is little light where I am, and my voice still isn't working.

My body cannot fight this force still pulling me forward. My mind isn't telling me to stop or turn around so I keep moving. Curiosity fuels me. I'm not happy or sad. I'm not scared, worried or excited. I'm numb. I move forward.

My pace picks up and I am racing again. How can I be moving so quickly? Thoughts do not last long here. They leave my head as fast as they enter. I can't hold on to any ideas. Clarity is not with me. All I can do is move forward.

* * *

Ten days later, I left the house at 5:15am to train a client. When I got back, I noticed I had left my phone on the kitchen counter. I'd never left my phone behind before, but I didn't think anything of it. My day had gone on as usual.

That night when Jake got home, he said, "We need to talk." He sat next to me on the couch, looked at me and calmly asked, "Do you want to be with me?"

"Yeah." I answered hesitatingly, a little taken a back as to the bluntness of his question.

"Or do you want to be with Him?" He said His name.

Oh, his face. Such a soft, sweet soul, but his face was hard. Serious. Cold.

I took a breath, knowing he had looked through my phone. Deflecting, I stated, "You looked through my phone."

He repeated the question, this time in a sterner tone.

Stubbornly, I repeated my accusation.

"Yes." He replied sharply. "Obviously. You left it on the counter and you've been acting weird. You come back from seeing Him and, suddenly, you want kids. I saw that you wrote that you think you might want to be with Him. So go, Lex. Go, if you want to be with Him."

Oh my God, he saw everything. I cannot describe the pain in his eyes that I had selfishly caused.

I replied that I didn't know what I wanted. "I'm very confused. I have no idea how this happened or what to do. I never thought we'd be here."

I have to say, one of the most amazing things about Jake is that he taught me not to yell. He's never yelled at me. He asked that I never yell at him. And so, that night we talked thoroughly about the situation.

We broke up. Got back together. Then I realized that if we were together, I'd have to stop talking to Him. I didn't know what that meant or what would happen if I stopped talking to Him. So we broke up again. I said, "I think space will be good for us."

I moved into our guest room for four months. I still talked to Him daily. He was a distraction from what I really needed to face—though I didn't realize that at the time.

I have to say that, as I sit here and try to share about the experience of living in the guest room, I remember, again, not allowing myself to feel or think too deeply about what I was feeling. *But,* if I had allowed myself to feel, I would have felt deeply sad, hollow and alone. It's very difficult to describe. I had never felt sadness that deep before and I'd never felt so alone. Yet, I knew I could talk to my family, but I felt foolish doing so as I had brought this on myself. I feared my family would ask me what the fuck I was thinking. I preferred to pretend I knew what I was doing and suffer in silence.

Some moments when I was alone, I would burst into tears. Chest-heaving tears. One time, I cried so hard I was screaming. I couldn't breathe, but I couldn't stop. Aside from falling in love, it was the most intense feeling I had ever experienced. I think what kept me going was knowing that I was going to be moving in with my sister in a few months.

And yet, I was surviving. I was exploring new things internally I'd never felt or thought before. I wondered if I had lost myself in my relationship with Jake. I wondered if I had been too influenced by what he wanted during our time together. I worried that I hadn't been secure enough to speak up for what I had wanted.

I thought I knew the answers. I thought I understood what was really happening. I kept a journal and, when I look at it now, I realize I was developing self-awareness. Awareness of the lessons that needed learning. One lesson being to establish myself as my own person. I had written a lot about being more emotionally independent and, though I had written about those things, I wasn't exhibiting behavior that showed I understood what it meant to really change.

In other words, saying I was going to do something and doing it are two very different things. I realize now that I had to learn that on my own. For me, that was rock bottom.

California, Here I Come

April 2013 – October 2013

And there it is, at last. A light. A view. An opening. I can see the trees part ahead and there is a clearing. I can see mountains, blue skies and white, puffy clouds. I can see clearly. With desperation fueling me, I pick up the pace and run to the clearing. I'm almost there....

Living with my sister at 29 wasn't so bad. Well, it would have been if I had let myself think about how I was 29, with no job, no money, no direction, no drive, and no self-esteem or self-respect. But, since I didn't let myself think about that, I was fine. I was living in denial and avoiding what really needed to be done. Yet, I justified it by telling myself, "I just need to see it through."

"It" being Him. I was still talking to Him; in fact, we were planning to see each other again. In the meantime, I did yard work at my sister's house to earn my keep. She was getting married in just over two months, so I also stayed busy helping her plan all the details.

It was a pretty uneventful time for me. I subconsciously stayed distracted by my daily dose of instant gratification and remained closed off to any option that steered me in another direction. I was self-medicating via text and phone conversations with someone who lived thousands of miles away.

That is when our relationship's true colors showed. What I thought would be a blissful time between us, sometimes became doubt, misunderstanding and disappointment. He no longer had a problem giving me attitude, telling me what he didn't like about me, or being short with me during difficult times. I hadn't experienced any of that in my relationship with Jake.

It's funny how family can be brutally honest and give you the messages you need to hear. My sister played this role for me quite a bit during this time, eagerly trying to help me see something I was not ready to see. When I would talk about visiting Him, she urged me to focus on myself, get a part-time job, and make Him "work for it." She thought I was too available to Him.

I understood what she was saying. It would have been the perfect time for me to explore being on my own. I hadn't been on my own since I was 21. I could've had some new independent experiences that would help me understand what I wanted out of life.

But, instead, I just stuck to my line about "seeing it through."

If Him coming into my life was strong enough to break up a relationship I had invested seven years in, wasn't it worth seeing it through to the end? Or at least until I was certain He was or wasn't my path?

Made sense to me.

One of the other activities that filled up my day was my daily workout. At the time, it was one of the best things I could do for myself. Five days a week of 30-minute interval spinning and three days a week of strength training.

Since becoming a fitness trainer, I had thrown myself into my workouts. I was in the best shape of my life up to that point. However, I was also scale obsessed. I weighed myself multiple times a day. Before I moved in with my sister, I wanted to see how low I could go. There was a lot wrapped around the number on the scale.

I wasn't anticipating losing so much weight. When I changed careers from teaching preschool to teaching fitness, I dropped 5lbs just by moving more throughout the day. I ate the same but exercised for 20 minutes several times a week.

Then, when Jake and I moved into our apartment in Henderson in September 2012, the weight dropped even more as I increased my training and ate less due to my long hours.

I weighed myself in the morning, after I worked out, after I ate lunch, after I went to the bathroom and before bed. Each time wanting to see a smaller number.

By the time I lived with my sister, I was 117lbs.

Moving in with my sister saved me from a very destructive path. I followed the same workout schedule but began eating dinner again and I gained 5lbs back. I also wasn't as concerned with weighing myself multiple times a day. So, it was an improvement.

I reached a turning point after my sister got married in July. My workouts decreased and I began to plan my next moves. I wanted to earn my Health Coaching Certificate in October, plan another trip to visit Him and other friends and family—which I felt I really needed—and finally decide what I was going to do in the next stage of my life.

By August I was making those moves. I was heading back East at the end of the month. My trip to visit Him was booked for September with a one way ticket (This was me, "seeing it through".) I planned to start school online in October. I just didn't know where I'd be living. It was the first time in a long time when I felt like I had just a little bit of my shit together.

Around the same time, Jake reached out to ask that I bring my cat, Oliver, back to my mom's. Oliver had stayed with Jake when I moved because my sister's husband is allergic. He had come to the conclusion that, "After all that you have done, I don't feel the need to care for your cat." I couldn't really blame him. So before my East Coast trip, I drove the five hours through the desert, to Henderson to gather the last of my stuff and fully move out of our apartment. Jake was on his own trip back East when I arrived, so for the next few days I had the place to myself. He had painted a few walls a very ugly dark green and had bought some new black-and-white photography, as well.

I packed. Boy, did I pack. I threw stuff out that, had I been in a different state of mind, I'm not so sure I would have. In my mind, I just didn't see how Jake and I could come back from this. I was sure it was over.

I put the remaining stuff in boxes, brought Oliver to the vet for his flight checkup, and got a ride to the airport for my one-way trip to Pennsylvania.

* * *

Oneonta

Green, lush trees surrounded me after landing, while humidity rolled through me and soaked into my skin, moisturizing me to my core. It had been eight months since I had been home. I had forgotten how familiar it felt to be there. My mom picked me up from the airport and, after dropping Oliver off, I went to visit two college friends in Oneonta, NY; the first stop of my whirlwind East Coast tour.

There was a sadness that came with being in Oneonta that I wouldn't let sink in. The State University of New York, Oneonta is where I attended and graduated college. It's also where I met and fell in love with Jake. It's where I fantasized about a future with him living the simple, quaint, country life in Cooperstown, NY.

Growing up in Connecticut, I always felt like I was on the outside looking in at my peers and social circles. Raw with insecurities and yearning to be accepted, I often disrespected myself to get approval from male peers. I wanted to get away from all of my insecurities. I wanted a fresh start where people didn't know me. So while most people stayed local, I ventured off to upstate New York. College was the first time I remember feeling at home in my body and, for the first time in a long time, felt I could be myself.

I remember the first time I walked onto campus. The feeling was unexplainable; but I guess that's what a gut feeling is. It was just right. I didn't have a doubt in my mind that Oneonta was where I wanted to experience college.

It made sense to me after that day why my gut told me to pick that school. It was where I met Jake, the man I knew I was going to marry three weeks after meeting him.

To this day it's arguable whether it was fate, God, the Universe or completely random how things fell into place.

It was days into my second year when a guy from down the hall came over to introduce himself to me and my roommates. He was in a band called The Forman, which often performed at a dive bar downtown. He invited us to a show. I wouldn't have minded going if the place wasn't so small and smelly. An even bigger challenge would be getting my roommates to go to such a place. So I lied and told him we'd go and moved on.

I was entering a heavy semester with Child and Family Studies classes and had decided to take an art class, as art was something that had always soothed me. I scoped out the room, as I sat in Drawing 101 hunched over on my stool waiting for class to start. It was an eclectic group. I could place a bet on who was a real art major and who was just there for an easy A, like myself.

And just like in the movies, his entrance was in slow motion. Tall, dark and handsome. Eyes dark like stones, and lush, thick curls peeking out from under his red baseball cap. A loose backpack hanging off his shoulders and a kiss of red coloring his checks.

I sat up. Art class was going to be fun.

A crush soon developed and, thanks to my roommate and what was known then as "The Facebook," it was easy to do "research" on the guy who caught my eye. Among other things that piqued my interest, such as photography and indie music, he the band name, The Forman, smack in the middle of his profile. *A supporter*, I thought.

Although I could have approached him in art class, I decided I needed liquid courage.

It was Thursday, September 8th 2005 and my roommates and I had plans to go out. They were even down to stop by The Forman show to see if Jake would be there. But first, we had other bars to go to.

As the night drew on, I began to accept that we were not going to make it to the show. It wasn't a surprise; it was definitely a long shot to get these girls to hang with a different crowd. So when last call was announced, I shot up from my stool and claimed, "I'm going to go!" They asked if I was sure and would I be okay to get home. I assured them that I'd catch the last bus and be fine.

After the show, I found the last two buses of the night waiting side by side. I was drunk and, in my mind, I was contemplating which bus to get on. Here was my drunk logic: *Well, you always favor your right, so take the one on your left.*

I walked to the bus on my left but it was so packed, people were standing. So I headed to the bus on the right. I walked on and who do you suppose was in direct line with my eyesight at the back of the bus? The tall boy from art class, with the brown curls that peeked out from under his red baseball hat.

Without hesitation, I jetted toward him and plopped down. I blurted out the words, "Hi Jake. We have Art together."

He smiled at me timidly and said, "Yes, I know."

I challenged him by saying, "You know me from class?"

"Yes." He replied.

During the ride, we talked briefly about class while his friend and cousin goofed off next to us. My stop approached and, as I stood up, so did he. It was their stop, too. We walked off the bus and crossed the street. The sidewalk came to a fork, and as he began to veer right, I wrapped my arm around his waist and pulled him left, asking him to come over for a beer.

His timid soul agreed and so did his cousin and friend. We had probably only walked 15 steps when his friend jetted out to the right and ran across the lawn toward his dorm. (This was typical behavior for him, I later learned.)

Once we got to the front of my dorm, his cousin looked at him and said, "I better go check on Kyle."

So there we stood. He followed me to my room. I got him beer and poured us both a bowl of Kix.

That was it. No making out. No sex. Just conversation and two nervous awkward hugs good-bye.

The following Tuesday in Art, we sat in our usual seats on opposite sides of the room. At the end of class, I was packing up my supplies when I noticed him watching me. I slowed down so he could finish packing up, too. We met at the door and walked back together, keeping the conversation light.

When we got to the fork in the sidewalk, he stopped and asked for my screen name (Yes, my AOL IM screen name). Back then, that was equivalent to asking for someone's number.

And that was it. We began dating. We fell in love quickly. Two years later we graduated college. Four years before settling in Vegas, we moved from Oneonta to Connecticut to Westchester County, New York.

And now here I was, eight years later, in our town. Without him.

No, I wouldn't let the sadness sink in.

Instead, I focused on my future and enjoyed being with my college friends, whom I had not seen in years, filling them in on the details of my life. It felt odd to share my story with them. Looking back, I'm not sure if it was because they just didn't get what I was going through, or that the situation no longer felt right after returning to Oneonta.

I guess it didn't really matter. I was doing what I was doing, and there was obviously no stopping me.

* * *

Connecticut

A couple of days later, I ventured down to Connecticut where I had lived from 4th grade up until college. Going back to what I consider my hometown is sometimes strange. It's where all my insecurities, teenage memories, happy family memories, and my longest friendships live. It's the place I wanted to run away from, yet always yearn to run back to. It's the state that drives me crazy, yet comforts me when I'm lost. It will always feel like home.

Visiting my best friend, Deonna, was like traveling back in time to high school. Over the years, she had become my partner in crime. If I killed somebody, she would have helped me bury the body.

This visit ended up being extra special since she and her husband were in a transition period and living at her Mom's, where so many of our good memories took place.

If there is anyone in the world who understands my history with Him, it's her. Coming from a two-day visit in Oneonta where the girls only knew me from when I was with Jake, to now spending time with my best friend—who so deeply knows my history with Him—only added to my confusion over where I was in my life.

She had actually been with me the night I met Him and featured in many of my memories with Him.

One night during Spring Break of our sophomore year of high school, we snuck out of my house. It was kind of a big deal as neither of us had ever done it before. We made sure Deonna parked her car on the street ahead of time, facing downhill. When we got in it later that night, she put it in neutral and we rolled down the street for a few houses before slamming our doors, starting the car, and meeting Him and his friends across town. We were out until the wee hours of the morning.

Oh, what is it about teenage lust? The butterflies, the excitement, and anticipation of seeing the other person again... And, when you did, your whole day would get better.

She was always the more grounded of the two of us, but we balanced each other out. Physically, she's short, with olive skin, long, dark curly hair, and brown eyes. I'm tall, blonde, with pale skin and green eyes. She was more reserved. I was more outgoing. She never needed to prove herself to her peers. I was always seeking approval. She held the same job all throughout high school, I bounced around until I went away to college. She always knew what she wanted to do when she grew up. It took me years to figure that out. She was the Yin to my Yang.

During this trip, I arrived at her house on Saturday and had plans to stay until Tuesday morning. We did a lot of talking, some working out, and drove by our old stomping grounds where our memories lived, including the two houses I grew up in. One of the best things that she was able to provide me with during this time of upheaval was unconditional love and support without judgment. She continuously reassured me that whatever I chose would be right, assuring me it would work out. She wasn't trying to help me see a different side. She wasn't telling me what she would do or what I should do. She didn't sit there in silence without offering support and love. She just comforted me and trusted that I would figure it out.

Empowering people to listen to their own intuition is one of the best things you can do for them.

* * *

Tuesday morning, I was off to visit an old friend who had taught preschool with me. She was living her dream life as a stay-at-home mom and running an adoption agency that makes it easier for potential parents to adopt children and babies.

She is one of the sweetest souls and I'll never forget the first time we met; I wanted to be friends with her so badly. She is the kind of person who, without even trying, makes you want to be a nicer, kinder, and more loving human. She and her husband chose to adopt after not being able to conceive on their own, and I loved spending time with her and her daughter, watching her be the amazing mom she was meant to be.

During my stay, another friend from our teaching years came over. She was pregnant with her first baby. I had known these girls for five years. We, along with another friend who had moved away, used to stand around on the playground together managing 24 three- and four year old's. We were all around the same age and would play practical jokes on each other almost daily. Some nights, we'd go out dancing until the wee hours of morning. We'd go to happy hour together after work. They were my first experience with "nice girls". We never gossiped behind each others backs.

They gave me hope for sustaining other female relationships in my life. They set a good example. It was heartwarming to see them all living their dreams: happy, married, and having families. I remember the many talks we'd had on the playground about life and where we'd be in the future.

Though it was great to see those ladies again, I felt disconnected. Not just with them, but with myself. Just like I did in high school when I was on the outside looking in. I didn't know it at the time, but that is what the feeling was: disconnect.

On my way back to Pennsylvania, I missed Jake; he was all I could think about.

What would your life be like if you didn't have kids? Why didn't he want kids? Do I even really want kids? Is that even what this whole thing is about in the first place?

My feelings for him began to thaw as I remembered the deep love I felt for this man. The beautiful life we had grown together. I began to question the intention of this trip. For the first time, I had a feeling of not wanting to visit Him.

But I talked myself out of that.

You need to go. You paid for the ticket. You can go home whenever you want. Otherwise, it will be such a waste and what if you regret not going? How will you know if it was the right choice?

So I stayed committed to going. I returned to my Mom's, did some laundry, packed and, the next day, I was off to the airport with my one-way ticket.

* * *

The Visit

The afternoon heat was scorching and I glistened in the humidity. I wore a long, black skirt and a white tank. My blonde hair, straight. He texted me that he would be a little late. When he finally rolled up an hour later, I perked up with excitement. I began to think, *This will be good.*

I walked over to his car... he didn't get out to greet me.

I put my bag in the back and got in the passenger seat. With a quick hug, he began complaining about the traffic and how much he hated coming "to the city." He had recently moved to a very, very small town to pursue his dreams and it turned out that it was about a two-hour drive from the airport.

I was bewildered as to his reaction. I guess it was silly for having expectations but, shit, I had just flown to see Him and He's complaining about traffic? I tried to downplay it and told him it was okay. I asked him to relax so we could catch up; He wasn't in that space. I took it very personally.

We made a few stops around town so it was dark by the time we set out on the two-hour drive to His place. I was quiet while I looked out the window at the night. He asked me a few times if I was okay. I lied and said yes. Then we were both quiet, listening to The Lumineers with the AC blasting.

Of course, nothing is ever how you imagine it to be in your head so, naturally, his apartment didn't meet the vision I'd had. Which was fine. I just wasn't expecting...

He unlocked the door, took a few steps, and flicked on the light. As I followed closely behind, he lifted his right leg, stomped his foot on the floor, lifted it up to reveal a dead cockroach, then swiftly kicked it across the room.

I stood there looking at the floor with my jaw open, aghast.

At that moment, darkness surrounding me, it became clear to me that he did not give a shit about me or, at the very least, he did not give a shit that I had come to visit. That heavy feeling sunk deeply into my soul.

I put my poker face on and pretended not to notice. I looked around the room. There was very little furniture: one chair, a tall lamp and a kitchen table that connected the living room to the kitchen. It was cold, lonely and unwelcoming. Which I got. He didn't need much, just starting off and all, but it did add to the emptiness gathering inside me.

He showed me to "my room" and bathroom. I rolled my suitcase in, using my phone to illuminate the dark, empty space. Apparently, there was no light in the room. Dead cockroaches lined the perimeter. I could not imagine the mindset of someone who could think it was okay to offer a room like this to a someone. I was in complete disbelief.

I looked at him and, as kindly as I possibly could, said, "You couldn't even pick up the dead bugs for me?"

"Well, you're not staying in this room."

"But you still gave me this room to use as my space."

"It's no big deal, Lex. They are all over the place here."

Yeah, I can see that. We have them in Vegas, too. You still pick them up.

It was the second time I had demanded my worth and he'd shrugged it off like no big deal. Boy, was He wrong. He was wrong. I was wrong. This was wrong. Screaming in my face. Wrong. Wrong. Wrong.

He asked me to join him in his room. I told Him I wanted to shower first. I felt unappreciated, alone and empty.

I tried to soothe myself in the shower. I told myself, *I can leave tomorrow. I can leave whenever I want, but I just need to try it. Give it a chance. It's okay. It's okay. It's okay. Deep breaths.*
Every feeling in me was pressing me to get out of this place. It was like I had something alive in me that was pushing and fighting to get out of my skin. An anxiousness that wanted to crawl out of me. I fought the intense urge to scream and release it.

I got out of the shower, sprayed myself with my Lily Pulitzer perfume, got dressed, and joined him. At a time when I thought I'd be feeling completely at ease and at home, eager to explore a new adventure, I never felt more out of alignment with myself.

We ended our night. I didn't feel alive.

As He turned out the light to go to sleep, I rolled over for a last check of my phone. I wasn't expecting to hear from anyone, it was just a habit.

There was a text from Jake.

"Watching *The Break Up*. This movie makes me sad."

I didn't respond.

I put my phone down wishing I was there with him. In our cozy apartment, in our bubble.

My heart hurt. I curled into a ball and closed my eyes.

Part 3: Waking Up

September 14th 2013

...and with my last step, I drop.

My breath leaves my body. The drop is long but fast. Looking up at the cliff I just ran off of, I notice it's getting farther and farther away, which only means one thing...

I guess when you fall that hard from a place that high, breaking is the only option.

Breaking hurts.

...Suddenly, I could feel again.

As I lay there looking up at where I had fallen from, the realization of what I had done hit me.

I was the cause of my brokenness.
I strayed from Jake. I was the one who left the path. And now, here I lay.

I need to get up.
I need to make this right.
I need to fix this.

Slowly, I come to all fours. Broken bones, cuts and bruises. I take a deep breath and move very slowly.

My voice works.

* * *

I woke up slowly from one of the deepest sleeps I'd had in a long time. So deep, I'd forgotten where I was.

My eyes blinked open slowly a few times.

Then my head shot up quickly as I remembered I was with Him.

I rolled over. Heartache and dread fell over me.

It became undeniably clear how off path I was. It was agonizing. I couldn't bare it any longer. I crawled out of bed, grabbed my laptop and began looking for flights home for that day. He lay there, just barely awake.

"Hey Lex," He spoke softly.

"Hi."

He turned on the TV and laid in bed. *All wrong, wrong, wrong.* Everything about this was wrong.

I didn't want to be with someone who watched TV in bed. I didn't want to be with someone who spent every Sunday morning watching more TV. That wasn't living to me. That wasn't connection.

Minutes went by before he asked, "Whatcha' doing?"

I looked up. It pained me to answer, but it also felt like it wanted to burst out of me. As if the sooner I said it out loud, the sooner I'd be teleported back home.

Quietly, I responded, "Looking for flights home."

"Really?" His voice dropped. He looked over at me, shocked.

"Yes." My shoulders released as my head tilted to the side. "I'm sorry. This just isn't right. This isn't what I want." I kept my voice gentle.

As I was writing this years later, I couldn't remember exactly what was said. I do remember sitting on the floor in his room, leaning against the wall, legs crossed in front of me, laptop in my lap, elaborating a little bit more on why it wasn't going to work. I was honest. I might have been a little too honest....

His guard was up. I couldn't see the disappointment in his face, but it must've been there. His family had invited us over for dinner that night. His coworkers had known I was coming in. And less than 24 hours later, I was leaving.

I called my mom and asked if she'd pick me up from the airport. I took a shower and got dressed. We grabbed breakfast at a diner then headed back out to the airport. I had tried to make conversation at breakfast, but he'd responded with a sharp intensity that gave away his pain.

"How can you just have a conversation like this? I can't just pretend everything is okay like you can, Lex!"

Later, in the car, he asked me, "What should I tell them?"

"The truth. Blame me. Tell them I felt it wasn't right."

From then on, the ride back to the airport was mainly silent. There wasn't much more to say. I gazed out the passenger window watching farm animals and the view of the plains pass by like a slideshow.

We rolled up to passenger drop off. He got out of the car and helped me with my bag. I wanted to say something concluding. Profound. Comforting. Something Powerful. Something that clarified a what was next for us. I frantically searched my head for something to say.

But there was nothing.

As he leaned in for our last hug, I couldn't believe it was over.

"Thank you for the ride," I said as I wrapped my arms around him.

"No problem." He released first. "Bye, Lex."

"Bye..." His name slipped off my tongue as I stood there watching him walk to his car. I thought, *Wait, that's it?* Still frantic for the right thing to say.

He opened his door, looked at me with his slanted, light-blue eyes and, before he got in, said, "Take care of yourself."

"You too," I answered, as my voice trailed off.

I walked into the building, up the escalator and over to the counter. I gave the woman my ticket.

"Um, Ma'am, this flight isn't here."

I looked at her panicked, "What do you mean?"

I was at the wrong airport.

Without thinking, I called Him.

"Hello."

"Hi." I cautiously continued, "I'm at the wrong airport. Would you be willing to come get me?"

"Jesus Christ, Lex, what do you want from me!?!" He yelled.

I squeezed my eyes shut. "Never mind. I got it." I hung up.

I got in a taxi and made my flight. I curled my knees tightly to my chest, angling my body to face out the window. I felt raw. Sad. Sitting there, staring out the window, not focused on any one thing. I had no idea what was next. It was such an odd feeling to not know what I was going to do tomorrow. To not know my next step, let alone what I wanted to do, where I wanted to go, or even how I would feel when I got there. What now?

My mom was there, waiting for me at the airport. I felt like a child when I crawled into her car, craving mommy comfort.

My mom is the best.

* * *

Pennsylvania

My eyes opened slowly. My head was fogged, my body was heavy and hurting. But I was home. In my mom's house. In my old bed that I slept in after I had graduated college. I was safe.

Writing this story, I thought, *How do I even begin sharing my journey of healing and rebuilding?* When I was going through it, I couldn't have. I didn't even know that it was happening.

Mainly, it was a time when I learned to be gentle with myself. To forgive myself, and others, if necessary. The awakening was great. But the healing and rebuilding was where the hard work lay. Licking wounds and mending the brokenness. Reflecting on the mistakes. The letting go of what no longer served me. The release. The moving on from it. The transformation. The growth. I had to actually wake up for there to be growth.

It's so important to be gentle with yourself during these periods. You see, when you're in this stage, you must remember that you're not the same person that you were before. I know this because the person I was before wouldn't be where I was at this point. I would have still been asleep to my life, trying to fit a square peg into a round hole. I would have still been looking for my identity in a partner, a guy to save me and give me the life I wanted.

But I wasn't. Because reality hit me like a ton of bricks and smashed me into the ground.
In order for me to get it, I had to hit the bottom—ya know, with all the rocks. I had to lose everything: my business, my boyfriend, my self-respect and my confidence (what little I'd had).

When you let yourself fall that far, it's impossible to go back to who you used to be. But you're not who you want to be either. Little did I know, there was quite a journey in front of me. That's what I wish I'd understood while at my mom's that September morning.

Though I felt safe, I also felt a foreignness within myself. I wasn't able to recognize myself or where I was in my life. It could probably go without stating that I never thought I'd be in such a position.

I didn't know what to do next. I needed time to regroup. I needed to let what just happened settle in and hit me. A year ago, I'd moved into an apartment in Henderson with my boyfriend of seven years and, now, I wasn't sure where I even lived.

When I woke at my mom's house, it was Sunday morning. I decided to just let myself be until I knew what to do. Though I did call my best friend to update her and I promised to keep her posted.

* * *

The next few days consisted of waking up to slow mornings of drinking coffee with my mom on the couch watching *Good Morning America*. I took walks with her and her French Bulldog, Lucy, in the neighborhood. I visited with my Grandparents and, most days, ended the day watching *Dancing with the Stars* or some TV movie before bed.

A few days passed. Then I finally saw what I needed to see.

I was there because I'd put myself there. It wasn't about choosing between two guys; I mean, come on, life is not a romantic comedy. Or drama. I certainly didn't want to be a damsel in distress. On a core level, it was about me. It was about letting go of the life I thought I was going to live so I could live the life I actually wanted.

Which was what, again?

I was sipping my coffee, staring out into the morning sunlight through the over-sized picture window, sinking into the cushions of my mom's forest-green couch, thinking about past conversations we'd had in that very spot about *her* life. I used to ask her tons of questions about her life: about when she was a child, when she was in her 20's, and what her life was like dating my Dad. I loved listening to her share. I was fascinated with her journey.

She'd had a very unloving childhood. She had been emotionally abused by her grandmother and her mother. She shared stories with me about the things they would do to her and the absence of love in her home. When she got older, she met my dad and they partied a lot, drinking and smoking pot. But as they entered their late 20's, my dad stopped smoking. He got into sales and they traveled, living in California and Georgia for his job, before having kids. To me, when I first heard this, it seemed so fun to smoke pot, drive across the country in a Volkswagen van, and not work. I also remember seeing a picture of my Mom hiking in Georgia. She was wearing bell-bottoms and her hair was shiny and beautiful, falling down her back.

I asked her what her life was like in that picture. She casually responded, "I was trying not to get a job."

I laughed and said, "Really?"

She followed up with, "Yeah, your father wanted me to work and I didn't want to."

I remembered how much that influenced me when she said that. I'd thought that I wanted her life. I can't tell you why I thought I wanted that. Maybe it was because she was the only female role model in my life and I wanted to be like my mom. Maybe it was because no one had asked me what I wanted in my life, so I didn't think to really ask myself that question. Maybe I just assumed my life would turn out like hers. I have no idea.

But parents can't give to their children what wasn't given to them. My mom wasn't asked those questions either, so she never really developed a sense of self until later in life. How would she have been able to provide an environment for me to discover my sense of self?

I was so unaware that my sense of self was missing that I had been moving through life in a robotic fashion. As I sat there, it began to hit me and I realized where I went wrong. Yet, it was only the beginning of my awakening. I needed to find out who I was because, as it turns out, I was not destined to be my mom. There was no way I was going to live a life similar to hers because I fell in love with a man who is nothing like my dad.

I had been easily impressionable when I'd been younger. My mom could have told me anything and I'd have believed it. This naiveté worked against me, as you can tell. But it also worked for me.

When I'd been 17 and my parents were still married, my dad moved to California for work. My mom and I lived in Connecticut, while my sister attended college. My parent's relationship wasn't going well. Oftentimes, my Mom would ask that I leave the house on a Friday or Saturday night when my Dad was in town so that they could "work on their marriage." She'd been trying to reconnect. I'll never forget the advice she gave me during that time of her life. We had been sitting at the kitchen table, and while I don't remember the context, she said, "Lexie, the most important thing to look for in a romantic partner is that he is sensitive to your needs."

I didn't know what that meant, so she went on to explain, "If you're upset, he holds you. If you're fighting, he listens to you. He doesn't blame you but you work together. He doesn't get uncomfortable when you cry in front of him or tell you to stop." I've never forgotten that advice.

It lead me to Jake that day when I looked him up on Facebook; His hobbies and choice of music revealed the depth of his soul and I realized that he had never truly disappointed me.

My struggle wasn't about whether or not Jake was the guy for me. I wanted to be with Jake. He's the most amazing human I've ever met. He treated me like gold. It was about the woman I needed to become, separate from who he was. I had never allowed myself time to explore that and I realized that I still had a lot to discover about myself.

My next move became clear: I needed to go back to Las Vegas. I wanted Jake, but I knew I couldn't expect him to just take me back. I knew I'd have to prove myself. I'd have to work on me.

He had a mountain-bike race in Big Bear that coming weekend. In the past, he'd asked that I go to some of his races and support him. I hadn't done that yet. I looked up flights home and texted him to see if it was alright if I went with him to Big Bear. And, just as if nothing had ever happened, he said yes. I asked if he would pick me up from the airport that Thursday. He said yes. It was an amazing feeling. As if I had found some land after being in open water. Some solid ground. I hadn't even realized I couldn't breathe before; I was just so used to it. Then, I felt the relief.

* * *

Las Vegas

I could feel it, the turning of a new page; I was entering a place I'd never been before. But I was sad to leave my mom. She is such a comfort and was so incredibly supportive during that time.

I was also eager to get back. I was clear on what I needed to do and I wanted to just get to it. I thought I was good to go. I thought I knew exactly what I needed to do and, damn it, I was going to do it all right now!

- Get back together with Jake. As stated above, he was not the problem. He never was the problem. My perception of myself and of my reality was the problem.
- Get a part-time job while I start up a new business–A girl's gotta earn money.
- Make friends and get out to meet new people.
- Get my certification in Health Coaching.

That's it. That's all I thought I had to do. (I actually laughed out loud as I was typing that.)

But that's *so* not how it worked.

You see, what I didn't realize is that I was in the "in between". I wasn't the caterpillar, but I also wasn't the butterfly. I was in the cocoon. In other words, though I had decided I was going to make those things happen, I hadn't realized the amount of inner work it would take.

> "You don't just wake up and become the butterfly. Growth is a process."
>
> –*Rupi Kaur*

It was Thursday evening, September 19th 2013, when I landed in Las Vegas. Jake and I were texting about where to meet in the airport. I was wheeling my suitcase behind me, looking down at my phone when he texted me to look up.

I looked up, my eyes searching through the ocean of strangers. Then I saw him standing several feet in front of me. Tall, with a huge smile. I felt myself smile, too. I began to move toward him as if I were being pulled magnetically, our eyes locked. When we met, I let go of my suitcase, I was unsure whether he'd welcome a hug. But his arms opened immediately. I followed his lead and we wrapped our arms around each other. I couldn't even remember the last time we'd hugged.

He held me tight and whispered in my ear, "My heart is beating so fast right now."

I wish I had recorded it because I wanted to hear it again and again and again. He loved me. He'd never stopped. And that moment when we reunited, he later told me he felt the same feelings he when we'd first met in college. I was Home.

* * *

So why do I share such a personal story? A story in which I was not living with integrity or honor, but rather, in denial and disconnect. One where I caused people pain. Why would I put this out there for others to read, judge and criticize?

I often asked myself that. But see, it led to my awakening moment. It led me to so many beautiful realizations. And as I began to share my story with others, I learned that so many people are suffering with similar emotional pain: feeling lost or stuck, and like they are not being true to themselves. Feeling as if they aren't whole. They, too, are unsure how to grow through it. They are scared of the process because they don't realize that the growth process, and taking the time to understand it, is actually what heals. And when you are healed, you show up better for the people you love and, most importantly, yourself.

So, yes, this is a *very* personal story I'm choosing to share. It's also a very real story. There will be people who read this who don't relate, and that's okay. Because for every person that this story does not resonate with, there will be another who is grateful I was vulnerable enough to share. Grateful for the knowledge that they are not alone.

I'm not claiming to have all the answers to life or that I've got it all figured out. But there are lessons I've learned that helped me not just rebuild my sense of self, but also how to be confident in who I am and who I want to be. Is that the answer to a fulfilling life? To know who you are and confidently go in the direction you want? Well, maybe not the complete answer, but I deeply believe it helps.

Part 4: Healing & Rebuilding

September 2013 – September 2017

The Desert Has My Heart

It was pure bliss walking to Jake's car. As if we had just started dating but had known each other for years. It wasn't officially what was happening, but the relationship felt new and comfortable at the same time.

I didn't get into any of the heavy stuff right away. All I wanted to do was forget about the past months for a few days and just be. I asked him if I could stay with him for a little bit and he agreed.

The next day, I woke up after Jake had already left for work and I went for a run. It was that day that I realized that the desert has my heart. I had missed the dry air; it felt like vacation air. Then, I remembered I could live here again. I feel alive in the desert. I feel like I can breathe. Surrounded by open views: colorful, rugged, layered mountains; blue sky; and abundant sunshine. I love the quail that run across the path on my morning runs. I love the different types of cacti that decorate the land. I love the Joshua Trees. I love the dry heat on my skin.

It was then that I knew I was going to stay in Las Vegas. Maybe not in Henderson, but I was going to rebuild in the desert. With or without Jake. But preferably with.

A New Perspective

We left before sunrise the next morning for Jake's mountain bike race in Big Bear, CA. I hadn't been up so early since I'd taught boot camp classes way earlier in the year. I forgot how peaceful and nice it was to be up before everyone else. It reminded me of the fresh start every new day brings.

We had just started the drive through the middle of the desert, when the sun started to rise over the mountains. There were hardly any other cars out, and it was just he and I on the empty road in the vast open greatness in the early morning light.

We talked about his racing and how it was different on the West Coast from how it was back East. We talked about how he liked mountain biking in the desert most, more so than in California or the East Coast mountains.

There is something about the healing process that is sacred. No matter how I try to describe it, I can never accurately describe the feeling to somebody. There is a loneliness, but also a hopefulness. I felt so free and full of hope, but yet fearful of what was ahead.

We listened to music in between our conversations. Lana Del Ray and Lord Huron always bring me back to the drive that morning and the feelings wrapped in that time. It was on this long, open road that lay ahead of us, that I knew it was up to me, and only me, to make the changes that I needed to make to get to where I wanted.

Jake is a great mountain biker. One of the best in your city. A total natural. He's passionate and he works hard at training several times a week. He landed on the podium for that race. It felt nice to have that experience with him. It made me want to have more experiences like this with him.

On the way home from the race I couldn't help but think, *What if we had kids with us?* In my mind I began to fantasize about two little ones riding around on smaller bikes while their daddy raced.

As I cautiously broached the topic, he was quick to remind me that we weren't even "back together".

I didn't like the unsettled feeling that began to consume me. I could feel that I was still attached to kids and life being a certain way. It was the only thing I was able to identify with; I didn't know anything else. I didn't know who I was unless a family with kids was the outcome. But I still wasn't sure if that was what I really wanted. I had just resorted to comfort once again. It was more comfortable to blindly go down the expected path than to find out who I really was and what I really wanted. And Jake had challenged me. I had to sit with that unsettled feeling.

Living with unsettled feelings was new to me. I felt uncomfortable not knowing what was happening. Where I was going. And so, it wasn't long before I brought up the topic again days later.

He had gotten home from work and I was in the guest room (my old room). After a quick catch up on the day, I broached the topic again with caution. Of course, that wasn't the only conversation that we needed to have. We needed to decide if we were getting back together or not. If we did, we needed to make sure that we didn't make the same mistakes again. How did we even get to that place to begin with? Was the issue even about wanting kids? If so, was one of us willing to sacrifice? I also needed to tell him what I had realized about myself and what I needed to work on.

Laying on the carpet, looking up at the ceiling, we realized it was not going to be easy. There was a lot to discuss and figure out. I also realized that such difficulty was new for us; our relationship had always been naturally easy.

The first thing I had to do was scary: I needed to apologize to him for emotionally stepping outside of our relationship. I needed to take responsibility for lying, for hiding, and for hurting him. And so I did. It didn't seem hard to own what I did for some reason. I think because I knew deep down that it was the right next step. In order to move forward, I had to take responsibility and I was eager to move forward. But I was afraid of how he would react to all of it. I was scared that he might not be able to forgive me or to move forward with me.

Instead, he forgave me. But he made it clear that if I did anything like that again, there would be no second chance. I was so surprised and relieved that he was able to forgive me so quickly. I hadn't expected it.

I reassured him that I would never do something like that to him again. I also stated that I wanted to get back together, but I understood if he didn't want to. I let him know of my plans to work on myself and to get a part-time job while I built a fitness-and-health coaching business. I wanted to let him know that I planned to pull my weight.

Then I asked that he take responsibility for not communicating his needs at the time. He had been struggling to take care of all of the bills alone but he had never talked about it with me. Withholding those feelings had contributed to the distance between us. He owned that part. Moving forward tentatively with the conversation, I asked him why he didn't want kids. He said, "I just don't."

It was the same answer he gave me in the spring of 2008 after we graduated from college. I probed deeper.

He explained, "I just don't want to deal with them. I don't want to give up myself or what I want to do."

I had never thought about having to give up myself for kids. I see now it was because I didn't have a sense of self to give up. So it didn't seem like much of a sacrifice. Eventually, the conversation softened. He was able to fantasize with me about the possibility. We talked about naming our kid after his best friend who had passed when Jake was 22. It was a first for him, to go this deep. To actually consider the possibility of it. A smile decorated his face while we talked.

The conversation turned playful. He lay on his back and held me over him, feet pressing on my hip bones and hands clasped together as he balanced my body over him. We joked about what fun parents we'd be. That we'd be on the floor doing this circus act and our kid would come running in.

It was nice to have that moment. And though I knew I couldn't hold on to it as a permanent decision, I was settled enough knowing that we had had that conversation.

The following weekend we went boating out on Lake Mead with Jake's friends. Jake had met Rob road biking shortly after we'd moved to Henderson. I had only hung out with him and his wife two times previously, so I didn't know them very well. His buddy had wanted a child but his wife had not. They loved each other very deeply so they'd decided to have one child. The wife is the breadwinner and the husband mainly cares for their daughter.

I remember one night when we first moved to town we had gone to their house for dinner and a game. Their daughter had hung out with us until she went to bed. The four of us had continued playing the game well into the night. The topic of having kids came up and they shared their story with us about their original difference of desire on the matter. They had made it work because they felt their relationship was more important. From the little that I had seen that night, they were a loving, sweet family.

I hadn't made friends during the first year we'd lived in Henderson; I had been too busy texting outside the state. So I was excited to see them again, especially after Jake and I had been through so much.

We'd started our day early. We'd packed food and plenty of beer and set off with Rob and his family. Eventually, and I honestly can't recall how this happened, we ended up on someone else's party boat. I don't know if the owner was a friend of Rob's or if it was a total stranger's, but there we were, drinking beers and playing beer pong. It was magical to let loose with Jake after months of being separated and in pain. It felt like we were in college again. Kissing and jumping on each other. It was bliss.

Shortly after we finished a game of beer pong, Jake's friend's wife asked how we were doing. No one in Vegas knew about the emotional affair. A few of my close friends and my family did, but no one else. Not even Jake's family. So I didn't go into those details but still expressed the idea that we might want different things.

And then she said something to me that, just like the words my mom spoke to me when I was 17, I'll never forget.

She looked at me in the eye and said, "You two have something very special. Something that most people are looking for. Most married couples don't have it and that's a big deal. Now, I don't know you very well, but if you leave Jake to meet a guy who wants kids and have kids with him, you may never have the relationship, spark, deep connection, chemistry, and love that you two have. Or you can stick with this very special, very real love and maybe you don't have kids, or maybe you do and you'll have both. Regardless, a love like this is rare.

This woman who barely knew me was giving me some of the realest advice I'd ever gotten. She'd made a similar choice. Based on what I had seen, she'd never second-guess her choice. She knows she made the right decision.

She'd seen us in them or them in us. She'd seen *it* in us. She'd barely known us, but she'd seen in us what few others had seen. My mother, my sister, Jake's sister, and some of our friends had observed that our relationship was uniquely special. My mom always described it like, "When you and Jake are together, your inner children play. It's beautiful. It warms my heart." I had felt that, too. I'd never known how to put it into words, but that was it. We play. And, after being in our company just a few times, this woman saw it, too. I knew that what I felt for him wasn't just my naivety playing fairy-tale with me. It was real. We do have something rare; she was right.

I held on to her words. I let them sink in. I took a breath and looked around at the desert mountains surrounding the lake, the blue-green water, the clear blue sky. She had given me a new hope. A new perspective. In taking in that advice, I learned to let go of my life having to be one way. Focusing on the issue of kids was distracting me from focusing on myself. Jake might be in my life to show me a side of myself that I wouldn't have found had I gone in another direction. A side of myself that's already there, just undiscovered or waiting for completion.

I started to consider that maybe it wasn't a sacrifice to not have kids, but quite possibly, a gain.

We're Back

The following weekend I went to California to get my stuff from my sister's and to update my CPR Certification. I was hunting for a part-time job in Las Vegas and an apartment in Summerlin. Jake decided he was moving with me—we were back!

I officially moved back to Nevada late October 2013—just in time for our eight-year anniversary. We celebrated by hiking in Zion for the weekend.

A few weeks later we moved to Summerlin and I started working at Lululemon. It was the first time since we'd moved to Vegas that I felt we were in the right place and that I was moving in the right direction. But, I still didn't feel well emotionally. I was raw. I felt sad and confused but I kept trying not to be sad and confused. I kept telling myself I was okay. But as I began to feel more settled in our new life, the past started to creep in.

He started to drift through my mind again. I thought it was weird that He hadn't appeared sooner, but I guess I had just been consumed with getting my next moves together. As I unpacked boxes, the thought of reaching out to Him entered my mind. I questioned it hard.

Why would I need to do that? Who is that for? What would I expect to come from that?

As I walked myself through my reasoning, I decided that it was me taking ownership of how our relationship had ended. I felt sad that I had hurt Him. He'd tried to back away last year, but I didn't let Him. I told him all was okay. Then we'd planned my visit, which I cut short, embarrassing Him in front of His family and friends. How could He not have felt hurt and disappointment? I owed Him an apology.

I was going to do it for me. As part of taking responsibility and a step toward forgiving myself. I had no expectations other than some closure.

And so I sent Him an explanation describing what I understood at that point about what had happened. I took full responsibility. I also asked him not to respond. And that was it.

Send.

Honor the Wound

Having taken that step, I was ready to focus on rebuilding. I threw myself into rebuilding my life and I got frustrated when it wasn't happening quickly enough—I didn't realize that I was healing and it was a process. I had the "I just want to be there already" syndrome.

I was grateful for my job at Lululemon. Being a fitness trainer, I definitely wanted to be running with that crowd—no pun intended. There was so much about working at that company that I needed at the moment.

It was the first job I had where people were genuinely kind and warm to one another. The company is also big on community and wanted its workers to work out at different places around town. The circumstances were perfect for me: I got out, met new people, and learned the area better. I was given free workouts at different studios each month and those experiences helped me make connections that have stayed with me for years.

I will say that exuding so much energy at such an emotional time in my life was freaking hard. Walking into a Lululemon store, it seems like everyone is taking happy pills. I couldn't bring myself to match their energy. I'd often wonder how anyone could be that psyched about life all the time?

I just chalked it up to being in a rebuilding phase. My lack of energy, of course, didn't always make it easy for me to be there. Years later, I would learn that during a spiritual awakening, people desperately want to avoid small talk and places where they feel the need to perform. I didn't push myself or make myself feel guilty for not being able to "show up" all the time. I'm proud of that. I think it is a huge part of the healing process: accepting where I was and what I was feeling each day.

I finished working at Lululemon mid-January 2014. Part of me felt guilty for not wanting to stay because I needed work and, being in the fitness industry and all, it was a good job to have. But the other part of me was relieved. I'd struggled to match my coworkers' energy and enthusiasm. I just wasn't in that place.

When healing, don't judge. Just let it be and do the best you can. This new way of thinking makes all the difference in the progression of your healing. As Gabby Bernstein says, "honor the wound".

Lesson 1: Our Wounds are not Our Fault but Healing is Our Responsibility. Healing is a Process.

These are the lessons I learned and the growth gained from my experience. I share the work I did on myself in hopes that you find some comfort and inspiration. Explore these lessons with me and, at the end of each chapter, take the opportunity to self-reflect and see what comes up for you.

I, of all people, know that life can definitely get messy when you're having an awakening. Stay with it and use the Reflections at the end of each lesson to guide you.

Awareness

Well, with no job, no sense of self, a new year in front of me, and 30 just around the corner, I'd say 2014 was off to a rockin' start.

A big part of developing my sense of self was understanding who I was. If I didn't know who I was, how could I know my purpose? The idea of knowing who I am or having a sense of self seems so basic, but it involves many layers. Foundational layers. How could I successfully accomplish anything important if the foundation of my being was shaky, weak or non-existent?

What I did know was that I was in some kind of pain. We only self-destructed and hurt others because we are feeling hurt or in pain. For me, a lot of that hurt stemmed from my relationship with my dad. For the first time, I decided to honor this wound rather than shove it down. I needed to take the time to heal and not rush the process, which was difficult. Dealing with emotional pain is hard. Most people avoid it. I know I wanted to. It was much easier to stay angry at my father than to try to heal the pain and take back my life.

Before I began this healing process, I thought trauma only stemmed from sexual or physical abuse or something violent. I quickly learned that trauma can be emotionally inflicted, as well. I suffered from emotional trauma in my relationship with my dad, which led to chronic experiences of not feeling safe and nurtured.

To aid myself in the healing process, I began studying spirituality, specifically Kabbalah. I had been exposed to a few ideas that had intrigued me when I'd been living with my sister, so I continued to explore it and remained open to learning more. Previously, I'd been an atheist and believed in nothing. You live. Random shit happens to you. You die. The end. I wasn't afraid of those thoughts. I wasn't raised practicing an organized religion. When I was younger I tried very hard to understand the idea of religion but it never resonated with me, and so, I resorted to Atheism. Until I was spiritually awakened.

The biggest thing I wanted to get out of studying Kabbalah was healing the relationship with my dad. That was my goal. Our relationship was the cause of so much pain and unhealed emotional trauma that I knew if I was serious about improving my life, I'd need to address it. I figured the more I understood myself, the better equipped I'd be to heal myself.

> "If you continue to believe as you have always believed, you will continue to act as you have always acted. If you continue to act as you have always acted, you will continue to get what you have always gotten. If you want different results in your life or your work, all you have to do is change your mind." — *Anonymous*

Easier said than done.

I read a few Kabbalah books and worked intensely hard with my Kabbalah Mentor. I could not have had the breakthroughs and healing I'd had if I didn't have his support. I think it was because of my dedication to healing that he went above and beyond what other mentors did. We'd grab coffee together weekly or close to and he'd coach and challenged me to go outside my comfort zone.

It was the hardest work I'd ever done in my life. I was often sick from pushing myself mentally beyond what I had ever done before. Not sick like having a cold or the flu, but more of an exhaustion. An intense feeling of needing to lay down and rest. I was literally stretching my conscious mind. I remember thinking, "This is ridiculous. Get your shit together." But when I tried to push myself, my body would only go so far until I felt the overwhelming need to lay down again.

It was only years later that I learned that such feelings are to be expected when having an awakening, as you are spiritually detoxing and expanding.

I'm not going to go into the specific work and study of Kabbalah because I do not think I could do it justice. However, I will tell you about the work I did on myself based off of what I learned and what my Mentor helped me with so tirelessly.

I was holding onto over ten years of anger and pain around mistrust with by my dad. I was a victim of his actions. And though my wounds are most likely not my fault, my healing is my responsibility. In my twenties, I used to spread negativity around like wildfire. Whoever would listen, I told. I played victim.

Playing victim is a dangerous and toxic path. It does not serve you or any relationship in your life. It's the perspective that things are always happening *to* you. A mindset that you have no control over the negativity in your life. You view others' behaviors as acts against you, rather than seeing that others' behaviors have nothing to do with you. It is a "Woe is me" attitude about your life. This is toxic because the more you tell yourself those stories, the more stuck you will stay. When you share those viewpoints with others, you contribute negativity to the relationship. It's also toxic because, as a victim, you are not open to suggestions of how to make your life better. You shut down other possible viewpoints and continue to choose to stay stuck in your own perspective. This makes it difficult for others to be around you.

It's not to say that you can't have problems and talk about what is challenging you, but it's the awareness that makes the difference. Everyone has problems and experiences pain; however, taking a proactive, solution-based approach can lead you through the process of evolving and growing through your challenges. At thirty, I was learning how to do just that and realizing that it was my responsibility to take ownership of my pain and work through my "Daddy issues."

I don't want to make this book about parents or where you came from being the sole reason you are the way you are. Instead, I want to focus my message on how taking healthy steps forward, regardless of where you came from, can enhance your quality of life. We all came from somewhere and it has affected us in one way or another. But we do not have to use our upbringing as an excuse not to go after what we truly want out of life. I believe with all of my heart that it is our job to develop self-awareness and make the necessary changes to align with who you want to be and the kind of life you want to live.

So, I'm not going to give the whole background story of my parents' lives. I will say that they, too, had great struggles as children that molded them into the adults they are today.

I want to highlight the fact that when you're healing your own wounds, you may want to learn about the wounds of those who've hurt you. It will help you to understand their struggles and, when you're ready, to forgive and have compassion for them.

That being said, I want to focus on taking responsibility to design where you want to go in life. So here is just a tidbit of what I had to work through and heal first.

There were a series of occurrences over my life that contributed to my wound and the unresolved anger toward my dad. It was the sum of all these experiences that built up over time and led to my resentment.

When I was around 17, I found out that I had a half-sister who was 15 years older than I was and that no one had known about, including my dad. It turns out that right before my parents started dating, my father slept with a woman and she got pregnant but never told him. She'd had a daughter: Jude.

At the time, Jude was starting a family of her own and her mother was curious to know the health history of Jude's father. My father. Jude's mom hired a private investigator to track down my dad. And there I was at 17 finding out I had a half-sister almost twice my age.

It was the first time I felt disappointment in my family. I'd been lucky to go 17-18 years being sheltered from "family drama", but unfortunately that meant I didn't have the coping mechanisms to deal with it. I wasn't taught to process what I was feeling. My dad just told me I needed to be okay with it, but I didn't know how to do that. It was as though my feelings were not important and I should just ignore them.

My parents' marriage had been rocky for years prior to the news. A year afterwards, they announced they were getting a divorce. Honestly, I saw it coming and I don't think I was bothered by it, at first. After all, everybody's parents were divorced.

It was May 2005 and I was getting ready to go back up to Oneonta to take some summer courses. My dad was living in Long Island and I still lived with my mom in Connecticut when I wasn't at school. She'd been trying to get me to call my dad because he wanted to start dating again. I knew he'd be dating and I didn't want to turn that fact into a dramatic after-school-special type of conversation, so I avoided the phone call.

As we were getting out of my mom's car one afternoon after running errands, I said, "Mom, it's no big deal that he's dating. I knew it was going to happen."

"Well, she's a bit younger, Lex, so he wanted to talk with you about it."

"Well, I figured dad would date a younger woman. What is she, like forty?" I was walking into the garage when my mom replied behind me, "She's 21."

I spun around screaming, "WHAT?!?!"

I was in shock. It felt like a nightmare for a few seconds. Like a total pinch-me, this-can't-be-happening moment. After that, it was a total shit show. The drama that ensued would've made for great reality T.V. The anger rolled over me. I called him names as I screamed out in disappointment. Rage just spewed out of me. I couldn't talk to him, I couldn't see him. I was disgusted.

What added to the anger and disappointment was that, according to him, I needed to ignore my feelings yet again. His response was, "You should be happy for me."

Reluctantly, I planned to meet him a month later to spend Father's Day together. Before I drove down for the weekend, we spoke on the phone to try to reach an understanding. My anger toward him softened because, as I like to think, I'm a pretty open-minded chick.

However, once I saw him, all my feelings bubbled to the surface again. I cringed as we hugged hello. I wanted to shrivel up into a ball and disappear under the couch. I managed to get through the visit, but then didn't talk to him for six months. I just didn't know how to deal with what was happening.

That fall I met and fell in love with Jake.

Eventually, I came around and I began talking to my dad again that Christmas. I was falling in love hard. I was grateful and I felt that my dad deserved to be in love, too. So I worked to move past my discomfort.

I met her the following summer in 2006; they broke up shortly after that and she moved back to Europe. He then dated more "age-appropriate" woman (including my Mom) but he missed her, and so, by January of 2008, she'd moved back to the States and they'd gotten back together.

And *just* when I'd gotten to a place of accepting that they were back together, he told me she was pregnant. And *just* as before, I was supposed to feel happy for them.

I just never got used to it. With every additional child they had, I shared less and less time with my Dad. Not only were my feelings being swept aside, but so was our time together. I would never get the adult relationship with him that I longed for and deserved. I'd have to grieve that loss eventually. It was made very clear that I needed to be happy for them. This lead me to believe that my feelings didn't matter.

This put distance between us and I began to emotionally shut down with him.

All that unprocessed anger and grief turned to resentment because I was not permitted to feel what I felt. It continued to grow inside of me throughout my twenties.

Over the next eight years there were more hurtful times. One in which my sister and I were accused of lying and leaving his wife behind purposefully on our way to our cousin's wedding. Though we were having a hard time adjusting to our new family dynamic, we certainly were not mean enough to have done that, nor would that be in our characters. Interactions like that only drove the stake between us deeper.

Today, I understand my dad's behavior. Then, I did not. That is the importance of healing. It is how forgiveness happens.

Over the years, I've written about this decade of my life many times. Sometimes it carried the tone of bitterness, hurt and pain and other times it was sarcasm and humor. As I wrote about it this time, debating over which stories to include to give a sense of how upsetting this period really was for me, I felt so distant from it. All this time I'd thought writing about it would set me free, but I've found that working through it and healing is what set me free. My perspective on it is completely different now. And like I said, the anger and pain from those stories feel like something from a lifetime ago, though the healing is recent.

But... before I got to that blissful place, I was angry at him for years and years and years. Some people would validate me and sit with me in my mud puddle, while others said, "Don't you want your Dad to be happy?" I fucking hated that question. It put me in such a strange place of, *yes I want my Dad to be happy, but not like this.*

More evolved people would tell me that I needed to *accept it*.

Why?

Forgiveness

I began to see why. My mentor would never let me play the victim card. My pain wasn't bad, he explained. I was allowed to feel it, but how was it serving me? How long did I want to sit in the mud puddle for?

At this point, it wasn't serving me at all. It was, in fact, keeping me from moving forward. It was keeping me from having a fulfilling relationship with my dad. The bottom line was that if I wanted to have a better relationship with my dad, I needed to accept him for the person he was. I needed to accept him for not being the man he portrayed himself to be and understand that he, too, is flawed, and that is okay.

I needed to forgive him for how he treated me. He was, in fact, doing the best he could with what he knew; just like the rest of us. I finally started connecting that the judgments I'd placed on him were the same judgments he'd placed on me with regard to my feelings.

"Did he have a right to judge your feelings?" My Mentor looked at me from across the table, holding his coffee between both hands.

"No." I stated powerfully.

"So, then why do you feel you can judge his actions?"

Boy, did I try to fight that statement over and over and over again. It was probably what kept making me sick, my resistance to releasing that. I was often sick for days at a time during this point in the process.

In order to transform, you must first identify the patterns that aren't working, the thoughts that aren't creating what you want and the emotions that are showing you you're out of alignment with your desires. I had to undo years of telling myself the old story and tell myself a new story, one that served my healing process.

I often chose solitude (which is very common when you're emotionally healing or having an awakening) while doing this mental work. I would go down spirals getting lost in built-up anger, just to have to work my way through and out of it again.

I also became increasingly aware of the two places people operate from: the Ego and the Soul Consciousness/Higher Self. I'm not talking about the Freudian Ego. I'm talking about the side of you that operates from fear, doubt, denial, shame, stubbornness, judgment, comparison, jealousy, envy, vanity, insecurity and selfishness. The Ego wants to receive for the self alone. It keeps you in a state of being stuck. It keeps you from light, abundance and your Higher Self. It's loud. You can hear it much easier than your Higher Self/Soul Consciousness.

Your Higher Self is who you really are. It's love, compassion, trust, authenticity, honor, security. Your Higher Self wants to receive for the greater good. It guides you to what you truly want to achieve, desire or attract and it's always about more than us. Most of us are not in tune with that voice because we function on autopilot and it's harder to hear that way: it takes effort to slow down, be quiet, and listen inward. But when you do, you'll hear what you really need to do to grow, evolve and earn more light.

You are always being presented with a choice: evolve or stay the same. If you choose to stay the same, you will remain in the same movie. Maybe with different characters, but the same lessons will continue to show up until you learn what needs to be learned. When you choose to elevate your consciousness, connecting to the strength inside you, and exploring what lies outside of your comfort zone, you will awaken and you will evolve.

During my healing, I also started to realize that the lessons we are meant to learn in life would repeat until we master them. Not as a burden, but as a gift, because it gave me the chance to learn how to heal and grow in love. Also, I learned that my pain is here to help me grow; my triggers are here to show me what I need to work on. I was forced to elevate my consciousness in order to evolve. And the outcome is a transformation where the the circumstances don't change, but the way I respond to them does. If I really wanted to receive more light in my life, I needed to work specifically on that part of my life that had been hardest for me.

That was my time with my dad. I did this very, very slowly at first. It was hard, but each time I presented myself with an opportunity to practice the inner work of empathy over judgment, I got better and better.

I realized it wasn't about what was happening, it was about how I was viewing what was happening. That's where my healing and evolution began, by no longer playing the victim. In choosing to overcome, I chose to learn and strengthen and to continue to chase the light.

There were setbacks. When challenges arise, as we know they will, the realization, first, should be that whatever situation you find yourself in is the one you need to be in for growth.

The setbacks were big. They would take me to dark places, and I'd have to do the work on myself all over again. Over time, I began to feel the changes. The setbacks were fewer and farther between and the rebounds were quicker and quicker. I could get myself back to a healthy mindset sooner and with less effort.

I'd visit my dad's house and feel lighter and less triggered. I'd leave without disrupting my inner peace. I'd gotten to a place of being able to take full ownership of my feelings and reactions and, when triggered, I acknowledged that those triggers were my problem not someone else's.

As I said, our triggers are here to help you heal and grow. That's why we have them. That's also why different things trigger different people: we don't all need to learn the same lessons. Putting the victim card away and taking ownership of our reactions is quite empowering. We are in more control than we think. And though it's work, and it definitely takes practice and a higher level of consciousness to do this work, it is absolutely possible.

One of the other concepts that goes along with this, is that while your triggers are your responsibility, other people's triggers are their responsibility. Don't take them on as your own. This is important to remember because as you begin to work on yourself and start setting boundaries with people, them not liking those boundaries is not your problem. You are not here to please others; you are here to take care of your own affairs.

We are also supposed to have big, scary desires, (for me, it was moving to the desert and starting a business) because our purpose is to evolve and conquer great challenges in order to grow as an individual. Our challenges are unique to our journey and our own lessons or karma; sitting on the sidelines is not what life is about. At any given moment we have two options: step forward into growth or step back into safety. It's always easier to choose the familiar and safe rather than foreign fulfillment.

It was at this point in the process that I realized what life is about. I was gaining purpose. Life is supposed to be uncomfortable and it takes courage to move down the path of healing and self-discovery. Embracing the scary shit that we are called on to do is our purpose that leads to fulfillment. When we share about it, we get the opportunity to connect with other human beings.

I am grateful for that awakening.

Grieving

Through this healing and forgiving process with my dad, I also finally grieved the end of my parents' marriage. I hadn't allowed myself to feel much back when it had happened. In fact, I distinctly remember not allowing myself to be upset about it because so many people's parents were divorced. It seemed the new normal. But normal doesn't mean it isn't painful.

As my mother would say, "Lex, normal is a setting on a washing machine. That's it." There is no normal.

No matter how common something may seem, it doesn't diminish the pain felt. My family broke up. That fucking hurt.

Looking back, I'd been grieving while going through the process of rebuilding, healing and working on forgiving my dad. I see it now when Facebook does throwback posts: "On This day...." I'd posted old family photos of the four of us during my childhood very often in 2014. I don't remember the feelings I had when posting those photos. From what I remember, I thought I was holding onto something. But maybe it was the opposite; maybe I was letting go.

The process took years. As mentioned before, there were setbacks and triggers. There were times I needed space from my dad for months at a time, all with the hope of getting to a place of forgiveness, understanding and acceptance of each other. I had to establish boundaries in order to further heal and to deepen my understanding of what was happening while protecting my energy. We both needed to let go of the expectations we had for each other and of how we thought the other person should show up. This work is well worth doing, though the journey is not always pretty.

"Transformation is dark and murky, painful and pushing. An unraveling of the untruths you've carried in your body. A practice in facing your own created demons. A complete uprooting before becoming." —*Victoria Erickson*

Remember, your parents are human and had a whole life of experiences that shaped them before you came along. And they, like you, are doing the best that they can from their own level of awareness. All you can do is focus on yourself, heal your wounds and do the best you can. I think that this is an important step to realize, especially if you want to be a parent. Break the chain. Heal your own stuff so you can be better a parent to your children.

Honor Thy Self

The healing process is no joke. When you take your healing seriously, a lot of unresolved shit comes to the surface.

In my case, the process affected my energy levels. My energy wasn't light and fun. It was heavy. This heaviness affected the way I worked out. I was used to spinning five days a week and strength training three days a week. For the life of me, I couldn't get on the freaking spin bike. I wanted to. I wanted to want to. But when I did, my legs felt like they were 300lbs each. I just couldn't muster up the energy to spin.

I spent a lot of time beating myself up about it. I would feel an insane amount of guilt and shame for not showing up in my workouts the way I used to. I needed to learn to be kind to myself and acknowledge that I was in a different place in life.

When I worked at Lululemon I was introduced to yoga. Prior to that, I felt yoga was boring and slow. But, now, yoga was all I could do movement-wise. My body loved it. It craved it. And it actually wasn't that easy at all. It required a whole different strength from me. What I needed most at this time was to heal and be grounded. That's what yoga helped me do. All I had to do was show up on my mat as I was and do the best I could. Hell, if I wanted to spend the whole time in child's pose, it was completely acceptable. It was soothing to my soul.

When my muscle tone began to soften, I became very critical of my body, especially since I was a fitness trainer. I felt like there was pressure to "look like a trainer." And again, I would try to get on that bike or lift those weights but my energy was still too heavy and my body didn't want that.

Over the next few years, I had to learn how to love myself for where I was. Old names that I was called in high school would resurface as I would critique myself in the mirror. I remember one boy whom I'd had a crush on had called me "Oafie." When I asked him what that meant, he said, "Ya know, big and tall." It certainly didn't sound like a compliment and, being 17, my self-esteem took a hit. But, despite those memories, I didn't want to be scale obsessed anymore. I didn't want to continue to be mean to myself. I wanted to be grateful for my health.

Over time, I learned to focus on all the good things I was doing for my body, like practicing yoga and putting healthy food in it. I was healing mind, body, and soul. I even stopped weighing myself every day. Not because I didn't want to know, but because my focus was elsewhere. I learned see that, though my body was softening, I was still very strong and my flexibility had increased. I realized that I'd actually been taking better care of my body than I had ever done before.

Today, I am even more accepting of myself and nurture myself more. For the first time, I understand how to honor my body for where it is. The relationship I choose to have with my body is one of love, acceptance and positive treatment. Yoga is a staple in my movement routine regardless of what my workouts look like. I feel healthier now than I did when I was spinning and strength training. Not that my old routine was bad, but mentally, I wasn't in a healthy place and the consciousness behind my exercise was not coming from a place of love. Movement is movement. Strength is strength. It doesn't matter what it looks like. It's okay if it changes over time. Your workout routine, just like everything else in your life, will evolve as you do.

A Different Kind of Healing

By the start of 2015 I had earned my Holistic Health Coaching
Certification and felt ready for a new type of healing— conquering
my sugar addiction. I had realized that I was eating too much sugar
because I was living out of alignment emotionally, but I was
unaware of how it all connected.

I originally became inspired to live healthier in college thanks to
Jake. He had opened me up to another world, one that I didn't value
before meeting him. A world that revolved around appreciating
nature and living life outdoors. Moving and breathing in fresh air.

I continued to struggle with exercise and healthy eating for years
after that realization. I didn't understand a thing about how food
was affecting my body: how food could cause silent chronic
inflammation, disrupt your gut health and affect your mood. I was
always on the, "I'll-start-over-on-Monday diet." By the time each
weekend would roll around, I'd already self-sabotaged in one way
or another. The struggle went on for about five years. It didn't help
that I was teaching preschool, where snacks and treats were readily
available. I was dealing with gut issues and constant bloat,
emotional eating, sugar addiction, guilt, and fatigue because I felt
unfulfilled in my career. I also longed to get away from the long,
brutal East Coast winters.

I would eat sugar as a quick hit to feel better or to celebrate the end
of the work week. It left me feeling even worse, as I would be
consumed in guilt and fatigue shortly after. I began to associate
sugar with certain activities: Fridays, weekend nights, T.V time with
Jake, or going to the movies.

It was a constant battle every single week. I wasn't taking care of myself or showing myself love and I wasn't building self-trust. Rather than questioning what the root cause of my habits were, I continued to give in to what was easy. I continued to model that I could not trust myself to accomplish what I wanted, then I would beat myself up for it. It was a vicious cycle of mistreating myself.

Emotional eating is okay to engage in from time to time or when celebrating a special occasion. However, when you use food or sugar to feel better because you feel lack within, it is not healthy. This is called eating your feelings. I, personally, didn't want to eat my feelings anymore. I wanted to release my feelings so that I could feel lighter.

By the time I was ready to address my sugar addiction, I'd already made important changes in my life: I had a more fulfilling career, I moved back to the desert and I began a spiritual awakening that helped me begin healing many emotional wounds. After these changes, it was much easier to control my sugar addiction because most of the root causes and emotional triggers were healed or in the process of healing. My health education also contributed, as I had learned how food affects your gut and brain health. I do not think I would have been able to forego processed sugar for a year had I not moved locations, changed careers, had a spiritual awakening and started this healing process. I had to do the inner work to realize that the root cause of my emotional eating was that I was living out of alignment with what I wanted, day in and day out.

Healing my body from my sugar addiction forced me to get real with my emotions on an even deeper level. I couldn't self-medicate with processed sugar when triggered. I was forced to go inward. In the end, I decreased my cravings by eating only natural sugars found in whole foods. That led to eating less over all because of the higher nutritional value in non-processed foods. I'd feel fuller on natural sugar versus processed and it settled the cravings for sweets. I was eating less out of emotion because I was healing the triggers and doing the work on myself.

After a year of being processed-sugar free, I occasionally still ate sweets but the intention or emotion was no longer coming from a sense of lack. And there was no guilt around my behavior. I was able to pass on treats when offered or when in the proximity of goodies. And I still can today. Freedom, Bitches. If you've ever been an emotional eater or been addicted to sugar, you know how freeing that control really is.

Health on every level can increase when you begin to understand you are worthy of healing and treating yourself with love.

Reflection

Awareness:
Suppressing your emotions will only keep you out of alignment with your true self. You may not even be aware of how that block is showing up in your life, so start to pay attention to how you react to things. What triggers you? If your reaction is not rooted in love, patience, or compassion, then question where that reaction is coming from. Awareness is the first step to change. We are designed to go through life feeling good. The only way to do that is to heal our trauma, pain, anger, and emotional wounds.

Use a journal to answer: is there something in your life that has caused you pain that you have not processed or healed from? Or that you do not allow yourself to think about? How do you think the suppressed emotion shows up in your life?

Maybe you don't know. That's okay. Just asking those questions and spending time with those questions can open the mind enough to connect the subconscious to the conscious mind, allowing the awareness to appear. Spending time in meditation after asking yourself such questions can also help bring the answer into your awareness. If you don't ever spend time trying to create awareness, then you will for sure never gain it. Even a little space to allow for something new can be just what you need to move forward.

Grieving:
Grieving is part of healing. Allow whatever it is you are feeling to come to the surface and release from your body. You may have to do this often; it depends on how deep the feelings go and how long it's been bottled up. Be patient with yourself.

Another opportunity to journal. Writing about your feelings can help bring them to the physical surface. Releasing your grief physically is vital to healing your mind, body, and soul. Feelings can manifest in your body in ways you can't even imagine. Trust that there is power and healing in grieving.

Forgiveness:
Forgiveness is also a part of healing and, when you forgive, realize you are doing it for you. It's common to think that when you forgive someone you are also saying that you allowing that person to continue doing that which you forgave. However, that is not what forgiveness is. Boundaries often coincide with forgiveness. They are how you can protect yourself while still having compassion, peace and love in your heart.

Forgiveness is an important step in your healing. Being curious about the roots of the pain source is always a good place to start. Is there someone you need to forgive? Perhaps yourself?

Use your journal to write about the pain that someone has caused you. You can then write about possible experiences that person may have gone through to lead them to cause others pain. I was able to do this work with my dad in person. I asked questions about his past and upbringing, which gave me a new perspective and allowed me to deeply understand where he had been. Not everyone will have such an opportunity so journaling about it can help. Meditation and visualization on forgiveness is another great tool. I never lost sight of the grand vision I held of having a good relationship with my dad.

Resentment and anger do not have to live in you. Forgiveness is the tool that gives inner peace.

Honor yourself:

Honoring where you're at is part of healing. Pushing is not going to feel good when you need to heal. Pushing yourself to be somewhere you're not will never feel aligned. Trust the process of emotionally healing and honor where you're at. That means doing the best you can wherever you are in your journey. I still chose to take care of my health even when my body didn't want intensity. I still chose to honor that health with nutritious food and movement, though my movement looked different. What are ways you can honor where you're at when pushing doesn't feel aligned?

Lesson 2: Having a Sense of Self is Vital to Our Well-being and the Foundation Upon Which We Build Our Life.

The Flight of the Hummingbird

One of the first things I did to own my newfound sense of self was to explore art and paint a mural. It felt good and it was something I loved to do as a child.

The mural was of a tree. Without realizing it, the tree was quite symbolic of my life at the time. I was rooting myself in Las Vegas, growing, branching out, and blooming. I painted the tree through the four seasons and, ironically, that is how long it took me to paint the mural.

I found myself wondering, *What the hell is my passion?* I married a man who, if he could, would wake up and mountain bike every day. I kid you not. He literally dreams about riding his bike. There have been many nights when he's woken me up, jolting from his slumber. When I ask him what happened, he'd reply half asleep, "I fell off my bike."

I started to feel like there was something wrong with me because I didn't have something that I ate, breathed and slept. I didn't have something that lit a fire in my heart and burned in my soul. Something that if I didn't do it every day, I'd feel unsatisfied.

And because it's commonly said, "Find your passion and follow it," I felt empty inside. As if something was missing.

It was at this time that a very dear friend of mine sent me a video from one of Oprah's "SuperSoul Conversations". It was called *The Flight of the Hummingbird, the Curiosity Driven Life* with Elizabeth Gilbert. I'll never be able to do this talk justice, so definitely search for it. In short, she speaks of two types of people: Jackhammers and Hummingbirds. Jackhammers are those who hammer away at their passion day in and day out. Those who don't feel they have a passion, but instead go from flower to flower or interest to interest pollinating each new endeavor with a bit of previous experience, are called Hummingbirds.

This distinction made so much sense to me. I finally felt I was given some clarity as to why I have so many different interests, and why I move on from some quicker than others. I had peeled back another layer and that allowed me to sink deeper into who I was.

Let's Take a Walk on the Woo-Woo Side

As I furthered my study of spirituality and continued to practice yoga, I realized I had a so-called "woo-woo" side, and I kind of love it! I'd never been exposed to that type of lifestyle before.

Real quick, I'd like to share the following... Spirituality isn't religion. You can be a religious person and a spiritual person at the same time. You can also be a non-religious person and a spiritual person, or a religious person and not practice spirituality.

Practicing spirituality is simply the act of elevating your awareness or conscious mind to understand yourself and others. It allows you to give more compassion and to live with more love in your heart. It involves taking responsibility for your life, your pain and your happiness. You can evolve as a spiritual being by focusing on your growth and consciously doing the inner work that helps with that growth.

Spirituality is not "woo-woo", though I understand that some spiritual grounding practices can be labeled as such. I, personally, don't mind the term "woo-woo" and such practices are fun for me.

I started to collect crystals a few years ago after I was given a few from a business coach. I was unsure exactly how to use them at first, but over time I started collecting ones that resonated with me. The more I learned about energy healing, meditation, crystal work and chakras, the more I wanted to leave my inner, uptight Monica Geller behind and embrace my inner, free spirit Phoebe Buffet. Stepping into my "woo-woo" side allowed me to peel off another layer of the girl I wasn't and to own what feels good to my soul. These practices (using crystals in meditation and manifesting) ground me in who I am and help me align with the energy I not only want to be, but also to attract.

I learned what the word manifestation meant and how I was constantly manifesting things into my life, whether I was conscious of it or not. Emotions are what create reality. These are all things I had control over.

It has been said that your thoughts create your reality, but I find that it's the emotion behind the thought that stirs up the energy in your reality. You don't necessarily need to change your thoughts, but maybe work to change your emotion around the thought. Here are some examples of what I manifested into my life at that time:

- Growing my business
- Peace in familial relationships
- My first home with Jake

Here is the thing with manifestation, though. If I'd focused just on the physical object, that wouldn't have been enough. I needed to focus on the *emotions* behind growing my business:

- What does it feel like to grow my business?
- What am I doing day to day in my business to grow my business?
- How does doing those things feel in my mind and body?

Of course, fear came up and I doubted in my capabilities, but those emotions did not serve what I wanted to attract. So I consciously chose to focus on the emotions I wanted to feel growing my business. Then I did the same for my next goal:

- What does the emotion of peace in my relationships with my family feel like?
- What does it feel like to go to my dad's house and spend family time together?

Maybe it's uncomfortable but why does feeling uncomfortable need to be bad? Why can't I embrace the discomfort? A lot of growth comes from being uncomfortable and growth is good. Finally, I focused on my third goal:

- What are the emotions of what it feels like to be living in my dream home?
- Not just what I want in my home physically, but what are the feelings of living in my home?

Then I had to act in alignment with the emotions of growing my business, finding peace in my relationships and living in my dream home.

This is a lot of work because we tend to focus on what we are lacking, what we are afraid of, or what we can't do. When you focus on these things, what kind of emotions come up? Fear, doubt, judgment, comparison, lack of confidence, unworthiness? These emotions paralyze and keep us stagnant, which leads us to repeat the same cycle. This is how our emotions, not our thoughts, create our reality. You are constantly manifesting your life, whether you are doing it consciously or not.

My relationship with my spiritual practices is vital to my well-being, as they keep me in an elevated state of consciousness. If I cared that others might think I'm crazy because I believe in energy work, I'd block myself off from the many miracles entering my life. I consciously choose my thoughts every day. I consciously choose to honor my feelings every day (in doing this I am giving myself what my dad couldn't give me: the acknowledgment of my feelings). I consciously choose to put out what I want back. I consciously choose to be the creator of my reality. That's not to say that I don't have difficult times or challenging emotions—I'll share more about that later—but when such difficulties come up, my practices ground and align me with all that I want to feel, be and attract. I no longer move through life like a ball in a pinball machine.

When you take the time to develop your sense of self and know who you are, you change the course of your life. You give your life purpose as you start to live from your values. You can't live from your values if you don't know what you value. If there is no awareness as to what you value, you won't find alignment in any area of your life. Something will always feel off kilter: a job, a circle of friends, a romantic relationship, a familial relationship, or even your relationship with your self. It's like pushing a wagon that's off kilter. It breaks down, it gets jammed up and it's super wobbly. You feel empty and disconnected from others and, more importantly, from yourself. That's what living out of alignment with your true self feels like. Taking the time to get to know yourself and your values provides the opportunity to make daily decisions that align with your true self and leads to a shift into who you want to be. You will begin to feel that thing that felt off kilter shift into place. Your ride will be much smoother. You may still feel some bumps, but your foundation will be stable and strong.

Also, when you honor who you want to be and the life you want to live, you will start to attract people in alignment with your value system. New friendships, perhaps a partner, whom you share deep meaningful, soulful connections with, all because you took the time to get to know who you truly are and what is important to you. Live your life from a space of authenticity, not seeking approval or waiting for someone to decide for you.

Don't be afraid to let go of what doesn't align with your value system, be it people, habits, thoughts, rituals, etc. Don't judge yourself for it, either. Just honor yourself.

Part of gaining my sense of self also challenged me to get secure in myself.

Reflection

Nurture yourself:
Part of developing your sense of self is to find things you love to do that soothe you. This is important in life as you truly are the only one to give yourself what you need. How often do you do things that are soothing to your soul? Can you do them more often?

Use your journal to make a list of all the things that you love to do, or would love to do, that would be soothing to the soul. Pick one and schedule it into your week. Protect that time. Show up for yourself every time you schedule a soul-soothing activity. Over time you will begin to build trust with yourself as you give yourself what you need, honor your boundaries, and heal.

Be Curious:
Don't sweat it if you don't have a passion. Just follow your curiosity and do what feels good to your soul. Stay true to yourself. Where in your life can you follow your curiosity?

Develop Practices:
Practicing routines, rituals and habits are vital to connecting to yourself and maintaining your well-being. Get to know yourself on a deeper level by having little practices that you do daily or weekly. Start with one. What's one small practice you can implement with ease? Write it down. As it becomes easier to show up for that practice, add another one.

Develop Values:
Find out what is important to you and what you value. Take action and live life in alignment with those values. Do you consciously live life from your value system? If not, what's one way you can start? Write it down.

Developing a connection to your sense of self is not about external labels or things. It's a way to connect within and usually happens when you are alone. Intentionally set time to be by yourself. If being alone is new for you, it may feel uncomfortable at first, but stick with it. Maybe it's taking a walk, hike or run in nature. Nurturing a hobby. Sitting in meditation. Journaling. Anything that is aides you in connecting to yourself.

Lesson 3: Getting Secure in Yourself & Owning Your Shit is as Magical as Not Giving a Fuck.

Limiting Beliefs

One step on the way to change is becoming aware of and releasing the limiting beliefs that are holding you back from realizing your own greatness.

Limiting beliefs are stories that are told to us from an outside source, or experiences we've had that taught us faulty logic. They *may* have served us at one point in our life but they no longer do. They appear as an excuse or a fear that we hold on to and carry with us throughout our life, limiting us from evolving and reaching our Higher Self.

They might show up for you in the form of an "I do or don't", "I can't", "I must or mustn't", or "I am/ I am not". Perhaps they show up in your beliefs about other people.

When feelings from the past are not consciously released, they get carried to the present. In order to transform, we must first identify the patterns that aren't serving us and the thoughts that create a distorted reality. Find the emotions that are showing you're out of alignment with your desires and purpose.

I remember the night that one limiting belief that I was subconsciously holding onto came into my conscious mind.

I woke up in the middle of the night and shot up in bed. In the pitch black, I stared in front of me and started crying, the phrase "She can't handle that" playing over and over again in my mind.

That was the narrative that I was told while growing up. Remember, I mentioned that in the beginning? I'd repeated first grade due to a "slight learning disability." I still, to this day, have no idea what that disability was. My mom just told me I could focus better in smaller classrooms, so I and a few other kids were pulled out of our mainstream class to get more focused attention.

From then on, the expectations that were placed on me in school were greatly different than those placed on my sister. C's were totally acceptable for me, while my sister had to pull A's or her ass was grass.

I vividly remember my mom telling me that I couldn't handle *that*. "That" being anything from mainstream classes, extra classes, working while in college, taking five classes at a time in college, etc. I got comfortable with this story and accepted it as my truth. It was my crutch. It was my excuse to not show up at my best. It held me back in life, just as it had in school. And at thirty, it was a pretty shitty story to be living in. (If I'm going to continue to be honest, at 34, I'm still in the process of undoing that story. I'm getting there though.)

That epiphany was powerful enough to wake me in the middle of the night. I'm so grateful though, because I couldn't change something that I was not aware of.

I was never upset with my mom for telling me that I couldn't handle shit. My mom did a much better job raising me than her parents did raising her, and I'm grateful for that as well. At the same time, I realize that this message was dis-empowering and didn't set me up for success later in life. It was time to release it.

Tuning Out to Tune In

I had to go through some other growth before I understood *how* to release my limiting belief and overcome comparison syndrome. Which brings me to my next point: when you're healing, there is nothing more important than tuning out in order to tune in.

In my case, I decided that I needed a break from Facebook. I took a year off and it was really empowering and healing for me to do that. It forced me not to get distracted by social media and allowed me space to reflect on myself and to be present.

Social media is loud. It has the ability to disrupt our peace more than we want to admit. It activates our subconscious mind and can trigger low feelings unless you filter out your news feed precisely.

It can trigger comparison syndrome: moms comparing themselves to other moms, business owners comparing themselves to other entrepreneurs, comparing your daily life to Susie Q's highlight reel of all the fun travel excursions she is doing. I've heard it all.

Or let's take politics and religion. They used to be taboo topics of conversation in public, yet it seems those same rules do not apply on social media. It's as if the ability to hide behind a screen has demolished all common courtesy.

It makes me wonder, is society really ready to handle the responsibility of social media?
The effects it has on our subconscious with its open forum for judgment and criticism is loud and disruptive.

It was interrupting my process of tuning in to who I wanted to be, discovering my beliefs and what I stood for, and most importantly, the healing I needed to focus on. So, I dumped it for a year. I gave serious thought as to what role I wanted Facebook to play in my life. If I returned to it later, what would I do to take responsibility and manage the feed to stay in alignment with the energy I wanted in my life?

I get that social media is great for connecting with long-distance friends and family, but there needs to be a balance: we need to be aware of how it's hindering our connection to our self and the people sitting right next to us.

I learned to do things because I wanted to, not because I thought someone else wanted me to. In doing so, I began asking myself what I wanted from life instead of living on autopilot. I began questioning my box of beliefs. I challenged myself by asking, "Are these beliefs mine or someone else's?"

Here's a funny example to give you an idea of how I used to be. When I was in middle school, I guess I wore things that were... a little out there. But I wore what I wanted with confidence. A classmate said to me, "You should be a fashion designer." So I actually went the rest of my youth (until I changed my major at 20 or 21) thinking I was going to be in the fashion industry. That story makes me laugh because, if you know me personally, you'd know I'd never feel fulfilled in such a cut-throat industry. I'm not a workaholic and I'm not competitive, nor did I ever show any interest in fashion. But when I was younger, I rarely questioned what people told me.

Anyway, as I dug deeper into my belief box, I found that most beliefs were from a family member or a peer; there were very few beliefs that were actually mine. I'd been carrying the fears or limiting beliefs that someone else had about themselves and had projected onto me. Which then led to the creation of my own limiting belief, a foundational one, at that.

I've been told I'm "too idealistic" and "live in la la land." So, any time I had a big, hairy, audacious idea, it wasn't truly accepted, supported or encouraged by others. That, in combination with being told I couldn't "handle" things, kept me stagnant. I discovered that my limiting belief was that all my ideas, dreams and desires were not good enough.

This had affected me deeply, crippling my self-confidence and sabotaging my dreams to own my own business and help others live healthier, happier lives. I'm sure you can see how damaging limiting beliefs can be.

As I developed my sense of self and peeled back all of these layers that didn't support me, I slowly began my transformation to a more secure person. It was beautiful. I learned that everything I'd ever needed was already inside me.

When you are in a state of lack, you see life through that lens. You see that you are not enough, that someone else has it better or is farther along than you are, or whatever story you may tell yourself.

But when you are in alignment with your true self, you see life in abundance and that you are enough as you are. You do not need anyone's approval or permission on how to live your life, what to wear, how to act, what to eat, who to date, where to live, what you should do for a living, or anything else that has to do with your life and not anyone else's.

Oftentimes when you feel insecure about what you're doing, you look for validation from others. Not advice, validation. They're different. Trust yourself. Take time to let yourself find the answers inside. You come on to this Earth equipped with all that you need. It just may not have been fostered while you grew up, so you don't know it's in there. But it is. So, trust yourself. You are okay just the way you are and you need to believe that.

What You See in Others is a Reflection of Yourself

This next lesson may be my favorite because it is empowering and freeing; it allowed me to separate myself from others' reactions and opinions.

Everything you see in others is a reflection of yourself. The good you see is what you like about yourself. The negative you see is what you don't like about yourself or perhaps an unhealed part of yourself.

Oh my gosh, when I began to apply this to my life, everything got good. Like, eating just the right amount of ice cream without feeling sick afterwards good!

When you own your own shit, it will never matter when someone else points out that you're standing in it because you already know it and, more importantly, take responsibility for it.

Let's take judgment for example. We all do it. But when we are too busy judging, we do not leave room for understanding, empathizing or loving. Those actions are mutually exclusive.

Here are two quotes that stuck with me as I worked on letting go of judgment:

"We don't see things as they are, we see things as we are." — *Anais Nin*

"I am not what you think I am, you are what you think I am." — *Charles Cooley*

During this time, I used quotes like this to help me transform. I found that if I judged others less, I'd have a lot more inner peace. So anytime I moved into a space of judgment, I caught myself and used quotes to help dig deeper into my psyche:

Where in myself or my life do I hold these qualities that I judge this person for? Or *What unhealed part of myself is this revealing in me?*

These are pretty powerful questions that held me accountable for my own shit rather than constantly pointing out others'. It's empowering because it works both ways: when I'm judged, zero fucks given because I already know my own shit. I can choose to work on it and change it or accept it and let go of that judgment.

Accepting yourself as you are is a difficult task in this world. It goes against our training, education, and culture. We are often told how we should be, not you are good as you are.

Acceptance of yourself first allows you to accept others and frees a lot of spiritual, mental, and emotional gunk, and the low vibes that brings energy down.

Judgment comes from a lack of understanding or a lack of empathizing. And if I'm not going to seek to understand or empathize, I need to mind my own business.

So, while my judgment of others says more about my journey, others' judgments of me say more about their journey. This understanding allows me to feel really fucking good in my skin. I can stay in my lane, focus on myself, take care of my own business, and own my shit. I really can't be bothered with what others are thinking of me or doing.

I'd like to emphasize that this is a practice. I'm not saying I never judge. I am human. I have morals and values and when people don't align with those, sometimes, depending on the severity, my reaction is judgment. Just because I know it, doesn't mean I always live it. I work hard to stay away from spiritual bypassing and to stay in a nonjudgmental frame of mind. I do the work on myself to live in alignment with this practice.

Owning Your Shit

I'm now so aware of when I'm judging that I admit it immediately. I may verbally get it out and then I ask, *why am I judging them? What do I know about this situation?* I talk myself through my judgment and it takes me off my high horse and forces me to own my own shit.

Do you see how that works? Owning your shit is just as magical as not giving a fuck. And not giving a fuck is a legit thing. There is a great Ted talk based on a book by Sarah Knight called *The Magic of Not Giving a Fuck* and another book, *The Subtle Art of Not Giving a F*ck*, by Mark Manson. If you don't mind, I'd like to put "Owning Your Shit" in the category of magical ways to live your life, too.

Another way to look at it is, nothing that anyone does or says has anything to do with you. It's a reflection of where they are in their journey of understanding and acceptance of themselves. People can only understand something and operate in life from their level of consciousness or perception. They can only meet you as deeply as they have met themselves. That's why it's important to remember that nothing anyone does or says has anything to do with you. It's never personal. Read that again.

Look at such occurrences as the opportunity to practice empathy in the sense that you could either choose not to care what they think or you could choose to empathize with them, knowing that they judge only because of the lack within themselves. I know because I've been there. Again, it's not personal.

I'm using judgment as my example to explain how to become more secure in yourself by owning your shit and accepting yourself. You can do this on other levels, as well. Everyone has insecurities. I've found my life to be easier and more enjoyable when I own my insecurities and work through them. When I own my insecurities, I can't be jolted by someone else's opinion of me. As I spend time getting to know myself and peeling back the layers, new insecurities come up. But part of becoming secure in who you are is knowing what you feel insecure about. Once you figure that out, you can then choose to change or accept it. It may seem odd to suggest that you accept insecurities, but knowing and owning your insecurities actually contributes to feeling more secure.

What does it mean to accept your insecurities? It means to allow yourself not to be perfect. Allow imperfection to exist in you. Know that there is always room for growth and to become better. That doesn't mean you can't like or love yourself as you are, but accepting that you are flawed helps you feel better on a soul level. We use a lot of energy when we live in resistance. Allowing yourself to say, "Yes this quality in me is not my favorite but, for now, I'm okay with this being where I am."

We are ever evolving. We are never done getting to know yourself, which means we're never done working through our shit. The more I let this sink in, the more comfortable I feel not having all the answers.

The bottom line is to stop worrying about what others *think* of you, how others *react* to you, how others *feel* about what you say or do, or whether people *understand* you. Don't worry about what others are doing or "how far along" they may seem in life. Let go of comparisons and worrying about being accepted by others. Get in touch with yourself instead. Focus on what fulfills you and makes your soul feel at peace. If you can accept yourself on every level, even what you don't like about yourself, you can change. Then you won't need others to accept you or validate you. This is the life-changing magic of owning your shit.

Reflection

Take social media breaks long enough to connect with yourself and others around you.

We can all benefit from taking a week or weekend off of scrolling and posting on social media. I believe nothing but good can come from regular breaks. I believe the harder it is for you to do it, the more you need it. Challenge yourself. Even if you start with just a day. One day a month. Consider slowly building from there. If that seems a tad too much for you, consider disconnecting from social media at the same time each night. There are many benefits to this: better sleep, connecting with your family/self, disconnecting from your day/work. What can this look like for you?

Challenge your box of beliefs.

The thoughts you have about yourself or things around you, where did you get those thoughts from? Are they truly yours? Are they true? Finding your own truth in your thoughts or beliefs is a way to deepen your sense of self and connect to your Higher Self.

Assess where in your life you seek outside approval.
How has seeking outside approval affected you? Have your ever
tried not seeking approval in that way? Practice giving yourself the
approval you're seeking before sharing ideas with others. It can be
challenging, but again, it only builds your self-trust and self-love.

Use your journal to make a list of the things you love about yourself
and why you love those things about yourself. Love yourself up,
baby!

Assess where you find yourself in judgment.
Next time you find yourself judging someone else, pause and ask
yourself, what does this say about me? Why does this trigger
judgment from me? How do I judge myself in this area? Is there an
unhealed part of myself being revealed? Reflect on it for a bit. It has
taken time for me to discover why some things about a situation
trigger me. Sometimes you don't find the answer right away, but it
is important to always own your behavior. Most times your
judgments of others will reveal how judgmental you are with
yourself. Seek to understand, not to judge.

**Assess the times when you're taking things personally
and making others' behaviors or reactions about you.**
Reread this chapter and practice putting the concepts discussed into
action when triggered. You can gain more peace in your
relationships, and in life overall, when you learn to let go of taking
things personally. Understand that what others do or say is a
reflection of where they are. Let that sit with you the next time you
find yourself in that space. It will help separate you from their
actions/words.

Lesson 4: There is No Comparison Syndrome When we Realize we are Mirrors of Each Other.

When I look back to when I restarted my business in 2014, I realize it was a little too soon. It was the beginning of my healing and rebuilding. I was raw and not feeling like a whole person, meaning that my foundation or sense of self was not solid. I wasn't done earning my Health Coaching certification, but I was in a place of "just wanting to be there already." I was insecure about what people thought I was doing with my life. Let's be real, nobody cared. Not that I didn't matter, but people don't really care. Nobody was sitting around wondering about what I was doing with my life. Those were my own judgments and insecurities that I placed on myself, rather than honoring where I was in my life. It would have been perfectly fine for me to continue to take time to heal and rebuild rather than rushing the process out of insecurity.

Indeed, because I chose to move forward, I was constantly in comparison mode with other women in business. It was a sure sign of not having a strong enough sense of self, though I was working on getting there. I was constantly coming from a place of lack within myself, which was steering me farther and farther away from my greatness. In other words, I was focusing so much on what other people were doing rather than focusing on my own journey and my own goals. I kept going outside of myself. But honestly, I wasn't capable of working on that at the time. I was busy working on the other stuff I've been sharing, so this insecurity stayed with me for about three more years.

While a distraction, comparison syndrome also brought me the opportunity to learn who was I as a fitness trainer. I hated going to the gym—in fact, I was never a gym goer. I preferred to workout at home. I wasn't interested in being ripped and taking selfies of my abs and I didn't want to sell workout DVDs. Could I survive in the heavily saturated fitness industry if I chose to advocate for health and wellness in a less sexy way? The pressure to stay authentic while still feeling a bit insecure was challenging. I found myself comparing myself not just to my old body (as mentioned previously), but also to other trainers. I compared my business to other trainers' and Multi-Level Marketing businesses, as their posts flooded my social media news feed.

One of the biggest things that helped me overcome my Ego, comparison syndrome and limiting beliefs was to go inward and get in tune with my Higher Self. I asked myself what I wanted in my business and what the vision was for myself? What was success to me? I love this exercise because it brings me back into alignment with myself and what I want, not with what someone else wants. Doing this in combination with disconnecting from Facebook helped tremendously because I avoided being shaken by outside influences.

It was when I turned 34 that I finally understood the saying, "We are mirrors for each other." I follow this beautiful soul on Instagram who is a yoga instructor and model. I paid her a compliment in regard to her yoga practice and how it influenced me. She responded with, "You see yourself in me." That's when it clicked. What I like in her is a reflection of what I like in me. Her yoga practice inspired me to move like her. I had that movement in me. If I didn't have it in me, I would not have been drawn to her practice. But I was.

Anything that you are drawn to and like in others, you also have within yourself—whether you've discovered it yet or not. Trust that if you see it in others, it exists in you.

What a gift that young woman gave me. I had heard it before but, this time, I was ready to *hear* it when she said it. After hearing it, I also came to understand how my comparison syndrome was blocking me from being able to see my own greatness. My insecurities made sense now: what I saw in those entrepreneurs on social media a few years back, those things I thought I should be doing, were in actuality things that I *could* have been doing. It is now the awareness that I see that in them because I have it in me. Inspiration over comparison. I needed to confidently go inward and pull it out of me with my own authenticity if I really wanted to do what they were doing and, if not, leave it and move on.

I began to make the same connection everywhere. I had been drawn to art since my childhood – heck, I met my husband in my college art class. Yet, I never allowed myself to own that I'm an artist. But there it was, sitting in me the whole time, my desire trying to pull it out while my limiting beliefs suppressed it. Because the story I learned to tell myself was that I wasn't allowed or supposed to make art.

Don't forget the contrast though. As stated in the previous chapter, you also see things in others you do not care for in yourself. And this is okay because we are human beings; we are not perfect. That simple awareness ensures you stand in your own shit rather than judge others for theirs.

It is rather difficult to release comparison syndrome until you feel secure in yourself. You are then able see that everything you admire in someone else you are capable of, and you already have it inside you. Have you ever experienced being drawn to something that someone else, maybe a friend, was not? The things you are drawn to are meant for you. When you see something in someone else that you like but you move into the state of lack by comparing yourself to them, it is an opportunity to turn comparison into inspiration. Go within. Make what inspires you your own.

Another common time when comparison syndrome shows up is in motherhood. I hear about it often. When you are busy comparing yourself to Susie Q and how she can "do it all" and how her life seems "so together," you dim your own light by comparing and being in a state of lack. Instead, observe what you admire about her and go within. Know that you have those same qualities within you, which is how you're able to see them in her. The difference is, she is acting in alignment with those qualities and she may be showing you how to do the same. She's not doing anything you are not capable of. If you want to show up similarly to the way she shows up for her kids—maybe she's super hands-on and does arts and crafts—you can show up in the same way. Or maybe you can be there by playing and running around in the backyard with your kids. Or maybe by cooking together once a week. The methods don't need to be the same, just the desired result: showing up more for your kids.

Anytime that you become triggered into comparison, try to use it as a way to begin the process of observing and going within to become inspired instead. The things you are drawn to, good or bad, are not random. They help you reveal your true self and take ownership of what you are here to work on.

I'd like to touch on one more thing before I move on. This may be more relatable to women or young girls, but it still must be said. Always choose authenticity over conformity. If you are drawn to something and your group of friends is not, never choose to conform over owning your authenticity. Denying your true self is a surefire way to live out of alignment and lead you down a path of unhappiness and lack of fulfillment. Be secure enough in yourself to own what you like and know that if someone is going to be critical of it, their criticism says more about their insecurities than yours. I wish I'd known this as a teenager.

"True belonging doesn't require you to change who you are, it requires you to be who you are." —*Brené Brown*

Reflection

Observe your judgment and comparison moments.

When it comes to judgment or comparison, it is truly never about the other person, it is always about you. When you compare, you are in a state of lack. The other person is simply the mirror reflecting what it is that you do or don't like about yourself. When you choose to elevate your consciousness and become aware of that and own it, you then have the opportunity to practice a healthier behavior that serves you better. Take the inspiration you observe and become your own light.

Begin to observe when judgment or comparison is triggered in you and practice using that person as a mirror to self-reflect. What thoughts or feelings come up for you when you try this? Journaling these thoughts or feelings and rereading them can help you understand yourself better. This practice can also help you hear something you were not aware of before, as you read your thoughts or feelings.

Lesson 5: It's not About Being Happy all the Time. Feelings are Messages That Need to be Explored.

In July 2016, something happened.

To be honest, it feels weird to say, but practicing gratitude didn't feel like enough. I'm not even sure if I'm phrasing that correctly. But for me, it was like I could practice gratitude daily, but something still pained me in my soul. Perhaps practicing gratitude kept me from spiraling down to a dark place during challenging times, but there was something bigger I needed to do.

I'll paint you a picture as to where I was in July 2016.

Jake and I had been married a little less than a year and we were living in our first house, purchased just five months earlier. A few months before we got married, I decided to take a job in corporate America as a work-from-home health coach. The job was fine, not aligned with my values in holistic health, but it helped pay the bills. Six weeks after we moved into our new home, a college friend came to live with us for eight weeks while looking for a job in L.A.

About a month after she left, I started to realize that I might be in a mud puddle. I was feeling the feels. The ones no one really wants to feel; those feelings many try to avoid. It was a deep sadness. A hollowing in my heart. A suffocating feeling.

Summer is one of my favorite times in Vegas but, during that time, there wasn't much I wanted to do after my workday was done. I'd just text Jake on his way home and ask him to stop at Whole Foods and bring me some veggie pizza. Then, I'd crash on the couch and watch Netflix. My soul was achy.

I found myself taking breaks from work to go into the backyard and stand in the desert sun, letting the dry heat beat on my face. I would close my eyes as I held back tears, mentally listing all the things I was grateful for:

- My good health (Mental and physical. I wake up daily with clean blood, a beating heart and all four limbs)
- Jake and his good health
- Living in Las Vegas and all the wonderful things that come with living here (one thing being abundant sunshine)
- Our beautiful home that fits our needs and vision
- Steady income
- The good health of my family members
- The spiritual awakening that led me on this path of growth and healing
- My friendships
- A car to take me from point A to point B
- The adventures I've had with Jake and the ones to come
- Our animals
- My future

I even wondered whether I was depressed because I couldn't seem to shift out of my sadness. Though it didn't feel as drastic as depression since I could get out of bed and function okay. I was just sad.

I began working with a Spiritual Coach. I told her about my journey, where I had come from, and how I was struggling because I thought I should feel happier. I told her the way I felt and that I was practicing gratitude but I just couldn't seem to shake the feeling that something was missing.

Through our work together, I learned that feelings are not bad. They are messages. We can use them to guide us through and help us get to the core of who we are. Feeling sad isn't bad. It may not feel good in our body, but it is there to tell us that something is out of alignment. Something needs to be healed. Something needs to be addressed. We need to be brave enough to go inward, to dig, and ask our self what we need to feed our soul. She was one of the first people to teach me that we have all that we need within us and that we are okay as we are, no matter what. You are enough.

So I let myself feel the feels. I didn't dump it on anyone else, I didn't blame, I didn't play victim, but rather, just allowed it to be there. I now know that if I don't try so hard to make myself "be happy", and instead stay open to receive the answers, what's missing will come to the surface and I will know what I need to do.

I was careful not to make my lack another person's problem and to not think of the sadness as my destiny. I knew that I'd get clarity and answers, but only if I gave myself permission to allow my authentic feelings to surface. I needed to explore what was missing inside of me to feel more long-term happiness.

So, I cocooned. I went from my home office to the T.V. I'd emotionally eat on occasion with Whole Foods pizza, and sometimes, I'd go out for a hike by myself or with a friend. I found myself living a lot in the past. Recollecting my childhood, a more innocent time.

It's funny how the mind will do that. Anything to not feel sadness or pain. It finds ways to distract you. But when you are aware and conscious of it, then you can work to control your mind and bring yourself back to the present.

After a few weeks I came to a realization: I am not made for corporate America. I was not happy in my job. My soul does not thrive by being placed in a box and being told I can only speak or be one certain way. Even just thinking about it now, I remember the ache in my heart as I would pull out my office chair and turn on my computer. It felt that my soul was dying a little every day as I kept acting against what I really wanted. I needed to get back to my truth and what I came out to Vegas to do.

This realization came in the beginning of August 2016. I decided I would quit my corporate job and relaunch my business. But I had to be sure that I was ready. I was not going to let outside shit affect me. I wanted to be sure I was grounded in who I was, aligned with what I wanted, and that no matter what, I'd move past obstacles and grow. In other words, I needed to be sure that my foundation was stable enough to relaunch.

I evaluated myself and found I was ready. I got my support team together and began planning my relaunch. I determined that I'd need a year to build up my savings, get clear on my messaging and branding and complete all other business-related tasks.

I had to give it to myself, though. I was pretty proud of where I was in life. I had gotten myself through a lot. Of course I had a lot of support, but my growth game was strong and I was so grateful to be at this place in my life. Nobody else can take you through a journey like this. You must travel it alone while loved ones cheer from the sidelines.

Finally, I could step into gratitude and feel that was enough. I wasn't necessarily where I wanted to be career wise, but I finally saw the light at the end of the tunnel. I had clarity and I felt a deeper purpose and a connection to myself again. I was grateful for what corporate America had taught me. I gained a lot confidence and expanded my skills, but my time there was up.

Choose Certainty.

Choosing certainty is a must.

I learned about certainty from studying Kabbalah. Certainty is an inner knowing that you are the cause of your reality and that you have everything you need to get where you want to be already within you.

It's consciously choosing your thoughts because you desire to co-create your reality. If you want to be successful, then you have to live in success and step into that every day. If you want to heal, then you have to live in healing and step into that every day. If you do not have absolute certainty that you deserve what you want, then the universe will make sure you don't have it.

The universe responds to clarity, not confusion, or cloudy, wishy-washy desires. Your actions are louder than words, so how you show up in the world daily speaks volumes. You literally send out vibrations and energy to communicate with the energy of the universe. In the end, you're not going to be able to achieve what you desire without certainty. You already have certainty within you; you also have doubt. It's your choice which one you step into daily.

If your attitude is, *"Well, nothing has worked for me so far, but I'll give it a try."* Then nothing will continue to work for you.

Certainty is not positive thinking, it's *knowing*. It takes you out of fear-based thoughts and aligns you with love and trust.

When you choose certainty, you're no longer at the mercy of every little thing that happens to you. You're in the driver's seat and you get to decide how you react. It's an elevated level of consciousness. And a powerful one.

So, I continued to do the work. Every single day. Choosing certainty. It was, and still is, a conscious choice to step into certainty daily. If I don't make the conscious choice to trust in myself and know that I can handle myself, doubt will inevitably creep in.

There were days when I wanted to quit the process and just get my own business going, but by denying the pull of instant gratification and staying committed to what I wanted long term, I knew I'd receive more light, more growth, and more reward.

Again, some days are easier than others; after all, we are programmed to have more fear than love and trust. But if you remind yourself to practice certainty and to tap into your desired feelings, you can consciously choose how you want to feel regardless of what's happening around you. It will help to stay in true alignment with yourself and guide you through the tough times.

Acknowledge the mud puddle but don't stay there too long.

July 2017, a year after my backyard breakdown of tearfully practicing gratitude, I left my corporate job and officially relaunched my business.

The biggest thing I learned from this chapter of my life is that life is not about being happy all the time and what an unfair expectation to put on our self. I had been striving to be happy as the messages I saw all over social media: "Be Happy," "Choose Happiness," or "Go Where Happy Lives" suggest.

And sure, we *want* to feel happy. We want to avoid discomfort and pain as much as possible. We all know it doesn't feel good when we feel bad. But the more we avoid our pain, the more suffering we are creating.

We are human beings; pain is an inevitable part of life. Going deep is hard. Feeling the feels can be painful and, perhaps, cause us to struggle. In Brené Brown's book *Daring Greatly*, she says, "We are hardwired for struggle." I believe that. It's just about what we decide to do when we're in the struggle. We are hardwired to overcome struggle. To work through struggle. To grow from struggle.

Believe it or not, we are designed and able to feel many different emotions, that's why we come with so many. We need to stop labeling feelings such as sad, angry, frustrated, confused, and any other emotions out there other than happiness, as bad. Instead, we need to slow down, allow ourselves to feel our feelings and explore them. They are communicating something to us. Something is not being processed, not being healed, not being released or expressed. Or maybe it is being released, and feeling other than happiness is a necessary part of moving forward. Or maybe you're going against what you really want, something in your life is misaligned with who you really are or what you really want. Feelings are messages and it is vital to our well-being to learn how to process them without judgment and use them as guides to live a more fulfilling life.

Toward the end of writing this book, I came across an interview with Brit Marling, the co-creator of a Netflix show, The OA, in which she discussed her experience working for Goldman Sachs. She is brilliantly creative and I was comforted by her story.

When she was younger, she followed her parents into the banking industry. She sat in a cubicle and worked very long hours on numbers that needed to be accurate down to the third decimal place. She questioned how so many bright and exciting young people found themselves there. She asked herself one of the big questions, "I'm going to die someday. Is this what I want to be doing?"

She explained the massive amount of work she was responsible for and the intensity of her job. There was no time for being sick. She also said that she often felt very sad. She would go home from work and sometimes just cry. Not just shed a few tears, but really sob. She described it as feeling heartbroken.

She went to see a doctor and discussed how she was experiencing waves of sadness and her doctor told her she was depressed and wrote her a prescription. She filled it but afterwards thought, *something is wrong here. I'm doing something that doesn't feel good and I'm being told that the answer is to pop one of these pills to make that wrong thing more palatable. To just go do the job. Numb myself.* Society's answer was masking the pain with medication instead of listening to the body's gut reaction.

She went on to describe how she felt she'd reached a place of dysfunction and couldn't bring herself to take the medication. That was the moment that she knew she had to find a new career; it was no longer a choice. She moved into the creative venture of film making.

If you're interested in what else she has to say, check her out on YouTube: "Brit Marling of Netflix 'The OA' had a Near Death Experience at Goldman Sachs."

Can you imagine feeling that way? So sad, yet staying in the place that makes your soul ache? What a horrible feeling.

Building off of feeling the feels, we need to stop sending the message, "Don't cry". I had a 19-year-old client who was obese, depressed, addicted to food and lived at home with her family. During family health–coaching sessions, my client would sometimes need an emotional release and she would cry. Her mother would then tell my client to stop crying because it made her cry. See, the root of my client's issues started with her mom, but her mom was not ready to explore where the emotions were coming from or in healing the root cause. She preferred to avoid the discomfort, thereby avoiding what needed attention.

We must stop being afraid of feelings and be willing to go deep. We must be willing to go deep. We must be willing to go deep.

If I'm being honest, I don't always choose to be happy. Some days I choose to hang in my mud puddle and splash that shit around, exploring and processing my anger or frustration or sadness rather than pushing it down and pretending it's not there. Sometimes I choose confusion because hanging out in my confused state helps me work through my shit and leads me to a world full of rainbows and butterflies. Sometimes I choose the mud puddle, but I don't stay too long—I don't want that shit soaking into my skin, ruining my clothes and fucking with my vibes. Basically, I learned to use my feelings as guides, messages, check-ins and opportunities for personal and spiritual growth. If you process them rather than shove them down or become victims to them, feelings can guide you on your path of growth and evolution. They can help you live in alignment with your true self and a fulfilling life—which is much more reasonable than forcing yourself to be happy all the time.

Life is not about being happy. It's about the process of becoming. In other words, get ready for this... Ready?

It's about the fucking journey. Boom!

I know it's cliché but, nevertheless, it's true. It's about becoming who you want to be. Shedding the layers or untruths or limiting beliefs or wounds that do not support us and evolving into our Higher Self. We can't do that if we don't process and work through our shit.

If you're serious about change, you have to go through uncomfortable situations and stop trying to dodge the process. It's the only way to grow. It's okay to be at a place of struggle. Struggle is part of being human, it's another word for growth. Even the most evolved beings find themselves in a place of struggle now and then. Struggle is a sure sign that you are expanding. The only one who doesn't struggle is the one who doesn't grow. Embrace your struggle. Know that on the other side of it, you will come out wiser, stronger and more evolved.

Please give yourself permission to feel the feels without judgment and let them guide you to what you really want. It's okay to not feel happy and excited every day of your life. In fact, most of us experience emotional trauma at some point and don't even know it because we think trauma only stems from violence. But that's not true. Trauma stems from a wide spectrum of experiences and, without processing and healing our emotional wounds, well, let's just say that shit will fuck us up.

When you allow yourself to question your reactions or feel what feels out of whack or feel what's missing, you get to know yourself on a deeper level. You give yourself a chance to shift into alignment with what you actually want to create in your life.

Going within, I met the only person who could ever heal me and carry me through my darkest nights: My Higher Self is a pretty badass bitch.

Reflection

We are not robots. We come equipped with feelings for a reason. Pretending that everything is fine isn't serving anyone. Getting real with yourself and honoring what's real for you will only help you feel better in life and allow you to connect to other human beings. Care about how you feel. Honor your true self and feel your fucking feelings. What do you think would happen if you did?

Good Vibes Only?

Let's get clear on what this means. This saying was trendy for some time and now I'm seeing people not understand it because it's not balanced with truth. "Good vibes only" means let's not shit on each other. Let's not be mean to each other. Don't be a rude asshole to the person behind the counter serving your coffee or give the driver that cut you off the bird because your vibes are negative. Take responsibility for the energy you bring.

It is *not* saying that low vibes are not welcome. It is saying that negative vibes need to be checked at the door. Feeling sad is not negative vibes. Sadness is just a lower frequency. You can feel sadness or lower frequency vibrations and still be nice to people — it's called taking responsibility for your vibration or the energy that you bring into spaces. Basically, honoring how you feel doesn't mean you have to be negative and spread negative vibes. Good vibes only isn't saying you can't honor how you feel. It's really about what you do when you're in that space. Let's take it further and talk about the law of attraction.

Law of Attraction.

The law of attraction is about learning how to differentiate between what you do and don't want. The law of attraction says to acknowledge the contrast, get more clarity from it, but then step into and focus on the vibration/energy you *want* to be/attract. Don't hang out in your mud puddle and live life from that space forever. That will only keep you in that low-frequency or negative vibration. You attract what you are, not what you want, energetically speaking. Use proactive, solution-based thinking to move you through lower vibrations and to help you gain clarity on what you want. That is why I say feelings are messages and they help align you with what you want.

It's okay to feel out of alignment. It's okay to feel feelings other than happiness—it's just about what you do when in those spaces. It is toxic to play victim and lash out at other people. It is healthy to own it and take responsibility for it. Move through it and grow.

Have you ever questioned what you felt or used your feelings as messages and guides? What do you think would happen if you did? What do you think your feelings are trying to tell you? Where do you think you'd go if you explored them? Are you open to taking ownership of your feelings and using contrast as a guide? If so, what does that look like for you?

Grab your journal and explore these questions. Have fun with them. Let yourself go completely. Then, when you're done, reread it to yourself.

Part 5: Fulfilment, Wholeness & Understanding what "Enjoy the Journey" Really Means

September 2017 – Present

It was a tale as old as time that I heard while on my own journey and it really resonated with me. Though I had heard the message before, it was only because of the place I was in at that moment of my life that I could actually *hear* the message. It took me another four years to *understand and apply* the message.

Here it is: Let's say you have a vision for your life, a place you want to get to that is currently not where you are. It's at the top of a mountain, off in the distance, but you can see it from where you are. Well, there is a journey you can embark on to get there. Trek your ass across valleys, woods, and deserts; get stuck in swamps; and hike up the steep mountain. There are going to be challenges along the way that may make you feel miserable and not want to continue. You can choose to see those obstacles as miserable or you could be grateful for the journey and challenges you overcome along the way because, with each challenge that you overcome, you are no longer the same person.

The reason I finally heard it differently was because on that day I was cracked open. I could understand what "life is a journey" meant: I was the person at the bottom looking up at my vision. I understood I had a long way to go to get to the top but I still didn't understand how to *enjoy* the journey of getting to the top.

What I understand now is that you have to actually start the journey in order to learn how to enjoy it simply because the person you are at the bottom of the mountain is not the same person you will be at the top. You may become someone you've never been or get in touch with who you've always been by shedding layers that do not serve you, or perhaps a little of both.

However, a journey of change requires you to do things you don't always feel like doing. For most of us, that requires delaying our need for instant gratification. When we live life on autopilot, we generally take the path of least resistance. When we live consciously, remembering the big picture or long-term goal, we are more likely to make choices aligned with getting to the top of that mountain, allowing our discipline, willpower and tenacity to become stronger. Transformation occurs.

Let's go on a journey together.

You are at the edge of a valley. Ahead of you is bright-green vastness. The heat of the sun elevates your energy and the blue sky promotes a calming belief that you've got this. You look just beyond the valley to see a thick line of evergreens bordering the far end and its difficult—nearly impossible—to see past those trees. You bring your eyes up now, just above the tree tops and see a large, tall mountain standing in the distance. The mountain is bare and jagged with snow-covered peaks. You can barely see a paved path. Your eyes are drawn to the top, where the sun shines lighting up your vision, your goal, your destination.

Around you are the many people you know. Some are friends, coworkers, acquaintances, family, and some are strangers. You look down at your feet and with a deep breath, take the first step. You've stepped on your first chunk of grass. That was easy. The crowd goes wild. You're excited.

An unknown amount of time goes by and you're sweating. It's hot, you're dripping buckets of sweat in the middle of the valley. You're desperate for shade. You can see a willow tree just a few miles away and think it looks like a good place to rest. You look to the side edge of the valley and the crowd seems to be just a touch smaller. Some of the strangers seem to have left. Your clothes are drenched and the tree isn't much farther.

When you finally make it, you rest in the shade. You talk to a few friends and family members about turning back. A few naysayers ask, "What were you thinking?" You think to yourself, as you wipe your face, *I'm not built for this.* Many would give up here. It's uncomfortable. But not you. You look at that vision again. It glistens as the sun lights it up and you notice that you have made some progress. Those trees are much closer than before, so you take off to cross the rest of the valley. You push through, feeling more refreshed with motivation and determination.

The forest is just feet away. The temperature is dropping as the shade grows around you. You stop to sit on a rock, chat with loved ones, and notice that the crowd is smaller. There are barely any strangers. Some acquaintances have gone and a few coworkers, too. You shrug it off, drink some water, put on a sweatshirt, and enter the dark, damp woods.

There are branches to climb over, thorns to pull out of your clothes and skin, Scratches to mend, swamps to sludge through, and bats to dodge. There are bears and other intruders to steer away from or fight off. It's long. You wonder where your crowd is. You can't see anyone; you can hear them though. You're tired of pushing and you consider turning around. It's cold and dark and the mountain is hard to see through the treetops. You stop. You look behind you realizing you're in deep. You can't see the valley anymore. Ugh, the valley. You cringe at the thought of the valley. You can't go back— you've gone this far. The end has to be near so you push forward.

The light filters through the pines and you can see a few people. You pick up your pace. When you reach the crowd again, which has gotten surprisingly small, you sit down and share your thoughts—maybe doubts, maybe certainties, that's up to you. There are still a couple of naysayers and you tell them, "If you're not going to support me, please leave." You look up. You've got a tall, steep mountain in front of you. There are a few trails: some more traveled than others, some straight up, some wrap around the back of the mountain. You're confused. You want the path of least resistance. You decide to figure it out as you go.

You think straight up the mountain is the most direct route and head that way. But it isn't long before your quads and glutes become sore. The dirt slides from under your feet. Your heart is beating out of your chest and you realize all the breaks you have to take to recover are slowing you down. So you choose a trail that allows you to maintain a steady pace. You can feel your body getting stronger, your mind is more hopeful. You pause for a moment and look down and back. You can see the path you've climbed, and out a bit further, the midline of the trees. Beyond that, in the distance, you can see the green grass of the hot, unforgiving valley. You think about the start of your journey. The excitement you felt, the people that surrounded you. You think about the struggle of the unbearable heat, the sweat that poured out of you. The thoughts or doubts you had. You think about the darkness of the woods. The thought of the cold gives you a chill and you shiver, remembering the wet swamp, the sharp branches.

You think about the push you gave yourself when you wanted to give in. The mental strength you gained and the pride you felt when meeting up with the small crowd along the way. Many didn't stay with you on this journey, but you kept on. You stayed with you on this journey. You're more than three-quarters of the way there. You look up. It's so close.

You feel joy. You feel proud. You're enjoying yourself. You realize you can trust yourself. You feel grateful. Through the last twists and turns and switchbacks, you discover that you like yourself. You respect yourself now and know that you are worth working hard for. You take the finishing steps to the top and the crowd has dwindled to just under two handfuls of people. The lovely few that stayed with you.

You jump up and down. You celebrate and hug everyone. You may celebrate later with dinner, drinks or a trip (maybe a relax-on-the-beach type of trip). Days go by and you enjoy the fruits of your labor. You enjoy the new house, the new weight loss, the new healed version of yourself, the new job promotion, the new relationship, the new business, the new clients, the new feeling of peace, the reconnection with a loved one, the second home by the lake. Whatever it is for you.

During your self-reflection, as you look around enjoying the goal you just achieved, you think about the person you were when you started. You make the connection that that person's mindset was different than yours is now. That if you were to embark on a journey like that again, you'd approach it stronger, maybe go a little harder, maybe stay more positive. You realize you've changed, grown, evolved. That those challenges in the dark woods were testing you and you passed. So you start thinking of your next vision, your next goal, the next level of yourself and you wonder how you will evolve from who you are now. How will you become stronger? How will you grow? What deeper version of yourself will you connect to?

While this place you're in is great and you've practiced being present and you're enjoying the now, you want to keep evolving because you realize that the process of becoming, though challenging and tiring at times, is exciting and fun. You realize that there are always going to be things you desire, whether they be material, emotional or spiritual. But the journey to each is about becoming. If you were already the person who could attain those things/qualities, you'd have already have them. And so, with excitement, you manifest the next thing you want to work to earn. You peel back the layers. You push when you need to push. You pause when you need to pause. Whether you're seeking to feel more grounded in life, to have more peace in a specific relationship, to earn a new car or a new house or a job promotion or a new healthy lifestyle, you must make the choice to go on a journey. To practice discipline. To go within and choose to trust yourself. The payoff is the person you're becoming. The relationship with yourself. The joy you're finding in growth. It is this knowledge that keeps you from getting so wrapped up in the chaos that you lose sight of the journey. Instead, you've learned to enjoy the journey. The destination is a highlight. The goal is a mile marker, the vision is your drive or desire. But it is the process of becoming, of earning, that gives you the real thrills.

I had to actually go through it to understand it. To connect with it. Before, it was just something I heard. Deepening my awareness finally helped me tune into it. You are not always going to be where you want to be, so why not learn to enjoy the process of getting there?

I'm learning to fall in love with the process and delayed gratification. Important things are revealed in the process. Show me the moment something happens; it happens in the "in between," not in the highlights.

Once I understood the process of learning who I was, owning my own shit, feeling secure in myself while feeling the feels, and trusting in myself, I started to feel fulfilled. And I realized what had been missing my whole life; why I had been so dependent on others to "save me" or make me feel good. Because I was not able to do it myself. Without having a sense of self or feeling secure in who I was, how could I ever be fulfilled? I hadn't even been aware that I was missing it. I didn't have the tools to overcome my triggers and challenges. I had been too busy allowing outside circumstances to control my mood and hoping/expecting/wanting others to fulfill me. The breaking point was the emotional affair. To this day, I have no idea if I would have woken up to a higher awareness had I not seen that relationship all the way through. Maybe, maybe not.

I can't be mad at that time of my life. I mean, I'm not proud of the girl I was. I'm not proud of how she treated everyone involved in that. But I'm not mad at her. She was empty and lost. She needed to learn how to love herself, trust herself and be her own hero. Those choices set her on the path to learning that. Having this awakening lead me to a life of exploration and self-discovery. I'm not so sure I would be living in fulfillment, feeling whole, if I had not had my quarter-life crisis turned spiritual awakening. The purpose of a crisis is to make you aware of the unhealed trauma that caused it.

Mission accomplished.

Fulfillment is a version of happiness. It's long-term happiness. That was the biggest overall lesson from my breakdown and from writing this book. Every lesson I shared here led me to fulfillment.

Feeling unfulfilled stems from living in a state of lack. Something is out of alignment. Something is missing. And rather than going inward to uncover our blocks or heal our pain, most of us think what we need is outside of our self. You may look outward to find an instant fix: food, social media, Netflix and chill, drinking, drugs, denial, defensiveness, an affair, validation, etc. Or you feel shame or guilt around not feeling happy, so you attach yourself to mantras and spiritually bypass, pushing your feelings down and ignoring the messages your feelings are sending you.

These lessons took years of work and sometimes I took much-needed breaks during the process. For example, the process with my dad was ongoing. There were some tough times. But with my new knowledge and the work I'd been doing on myself, it was different. I was different. I could practice the beliefs I learned about compassion, not judging, and acceptance.

However, it became really challenging at times. I'd take a step back from my dad and our work, and that was okay, because I knew I was doing my part. I was honoring my self-worth. I was practicing compassion *and* boundaries. I was doing the work on myself to change my own behavior and the rest was out of my control.

Going inward won't result in instant gratification. But, eventually, as you get to know yourself, it will become more gratifying, because it will not provide short-term happiness, but rather, the tools needed to sustain soothing, long-term happiness, known as fulfillment.

When I began living in fulfillment, I began feeling whole. The thing I hadn't realized was that it was accessible to me the whole time. Just as it is accessible to you now. You have to heal the trauma and peel back the blocks and limiting beliefs that interrupt your vision and growth.

In the last half of 2017 I took my journey deeper, allowing myself to live in fulfillment by doing things that connected me to my inner self. I started painting regularly and sharing it, not really worried if I was good or not. I was not attached to any one specific outcome, just doing it because it felt good and it helped me stay present.

I also started taking my writing more seriously, allowed myself more time for gardening, and stepped into woo-woo hippy-dippy rituals that grounded me even more. I moved my body on a consistent basis. I nourished my need for going deep by having soulful conversations about spiritual growth, healing and self-development. I learned to love and honor both the fact that I'm *not* a workaholic but I have a love for diamonds.

Stepping into who you are and owning yourself fully is a major step in feeling fulfilled. Even owning that you don't always know who you are will lead to fulfillment. I would never have been able to live in fulfillment had I not taken the time to heal and rebuild my foundation. I needed to reintroduce myself to myself. I learned that all I need to do is live authentically, vulnerably and consciously, as best I can. I don't need to wake up every day with the sun shining out my bum and rainbows and butterflies springing from my bed (though that happens for me now more times than not). I can bravely honor my feelings and use them to guide me to live in alignment with my true self. Feeling fulfilled and whole comes from within, regardless of what's happening around me, and I can view my triggers as opportunities that empower me to grow.

Healing leads to self-love. The idea of self-love seems so fucking simple. Over the years, I'd heard people talk about it all the time, but I found it wasn't that simple for me and I didn't understand what it meant. I would ask myself, *Do I love myself? What the hell does it mean to love yourself? How do you do that?*

It hit me one summer afternoon in 2018, this time a backyard breakthrough. I was standing in the August desert heat, working on a backyard project with my incredible husband. I stood reflecting on how far we'd come—how far I'd come—when I realized I liked who I was. I didn't need validation from family members anymore. I didn't need stimulation or validation via social media. I didn't feel that I needed to share everything I was doing. I was fulfilled in simply connecting with myself. I was deeply happy just being.

I was also happy being by myself. I was loving all the things I was discovering about myself. I felt like I had truly transformed because I was showing up in alignment with the vision I'd had in my head for years. And what I had been putting into practice for the last four years was now a part of who I was. I learned to trust myself. I was proud of myself for becoming this woman—with the support of others—but really, this is a journey I went on by myself. And I realized in the middle of my dusty, messy backyard, in my sweaty sun-kissed body: *Fuck...* this *is what loving yourself is.* I wasn't treading water in the middle of the ocean. I wasn't clinging to a buoy. I wasn't alone on an island. I had gotten myself home.

Final Reflections

Practice Self-Awareness

Society does not teach us how to connect with our self, how to take care of our emotional well-being, or how to develop self-awareness. We are not taught about the importance of these things in school, so we grow up not understanding how to live fulfilled lives with acceptance and connection to who we really are.

Instead, we think we need things outside of our self to bring us happiness, be it a relationship or something material. We opt for quick hits, short-term bursts to get us by. And when that's over, we are left thinking there is something wrong with us because our happiness isn't lasting. We don't understand that it's about going deeper.

It took me four years of rebuilding to learn that my lessons were about more than happiness. I'd been avoiding the most important work: the work on myself that would lead to true fulfillment. The work to heal, learn about myself, and grow. The work to develop more self-awareness around how I showed up in the world.

You can't change what you're not aware of. Every human has a different degree of awareness. The more self-aware you choose to become, the more likely you are to evolve toward the human you want to be. And then, believe it or not, life becomes easier, emotionally and physically.

The connection or relationship we have with our self is the foundation of our emotional well being. Our emotional well-being will set the stage for our physical well-being. Health starts with the relationship we have with our self. If we focus on your emotional wellness first, it can make the path to physical wellness easier.

I was listening to The Resist Average Academy Podcast and Tommy Baker was interviewing someone. I can not remember his name but he stated this, "You live lives as adults created by children. Connect with that and then stop making excuses for it." My mom used to tell me, "You can't give to somebody, what wasn't given to you." What I have learned through my own journey of healing is that YOU *must learn to give yourself what wasn't given to you.* This is how you'll be able to give it to others. When you love yourself, you will feel complete. When you're complete, what else is there to do but be in service to others? Be a chain breaker. Stop the cycle. It is our responsibility to heal our wounds. Especially if we decide to have children. We must be willing to go deep within our self. Be who you needed when you were younger. Heal yourself.

But we can't heal in the same environment that made us sick or hurt us. In order to heal and truly transform our life, we must change our subconscious programming. It's our inability to conceive things that holds us back. What I learned is that it's not really about adding in new things (though sometimes it will be), it's more about letting go of beliefs or things that don't serve us. Things that are not in alignment with where you want to go or who you want to be.

These are not new ideas, people have been talking about these concepts for decades. The thing is, we can't always hear them. We can only understand and comprehend from the level of consciousness that we are awake to. So while we may have heard similar thoughts before, we only understood them from the level we are at. You may read this book, years later find yourself in a different place in life, read this book again, only to hear a message you didn't truly hear before. It happens all the time when you live life with an open, ever-evolving mindset. In that space, healing, connection and fulfillment can take place.

First, build deeper self-awareness around your emotional well-being. Become aware of whether you allow people or circumstances to affect your mood or how you feel about yourself. Use a journal to write down what bothers you and why. Reflect on where you think this might stem from. You might find there is some inner work around healing that needs to be done. This is part of noticing the messages/lessons.

Lessons and opportunity for healing and growth do not show up in life in a way that makes us feel good. When our Ego shows up (fear, doubt, jealousy, anger, disappointment, judgment, etc.), remember that our Ego is not who we are. Our Ego keeps us from being who we are meant to be. If you can take the time to pause and reflect on what's really happening, you'll find that the universe is sending you a message around an area that you need to heal and grow from. It is an opportunity to change your perspective and be grateful for the experience as it's helping you evolve into your Higher Self. This is what true gratitude is: being grateful when things are hard because you understand it's for your higher good. Being grateful during a challenging time instead of just when things are going your way.

Also, work on creating a safe space for yourself. There are certain places where it is inappropriate to emotionally fall apart and splash around in your mud puddle. That's why it's so important to create a close circle of support to give you the space to release. When you take the time to go inward, you can never go wrong. Tuning in and listening to those uncomfortable feelings for guidance sometimes is the very best thing you can do for yourself. Take the pressure off and honor those feelings that are coming up for you at the time. It could very well be the secret to accepting yourself and loving yourself as is.

Third, build awareness of what you value. Creating this awareness is a great place to start focusing on where to make changes. Write down your values in all areas of your life. Reflect on where your current life matches your values. Identify where your life doesn't match your values. Shift accordingly.

The Never-Ending Growth Game

Keep in mind we are never done doing our work. It was said to me once, "As long as you're alive, you have work to do." But as you get better at your growth game, the work becomes a little easier because you've gained the tools to help you stay in alignment. I'm not always living in alignment, and when I recognize that I've slipped, I dig around in my toolbox to find the practice that gives me the shift I need to get back on track.

So remember, we're never done. We are always evolving. We will be tested in our growth and will need maintenance work to help keep ourselves in check. That's okay, so don't be hard on yourself about that. Contrast in life is okay.

Right now, I'm in the process of learning to let go and not be so hard on myself for the girl I used to be. To be honest, I don't speak very lovingly about her when I share about her. I even speak about her in the third person, as if I'm completely detached from her. Though I am not mad or angry with my past self, I don't think very highly of my unevolved self. But I'm trying to accept and forgive that girl because she brought me to be the woman I am today. She was in pain because she didn't know who she was and didn't respect herself. That is why I'm not mad at her and understand the need to love her. I need to also realize that she's still very much a part of me today. She still has the fun, loving, silly qualities. She is just more evolved now. More mature… wiser… grounded.

What's difficult for me to accept are the cringeworthy moments when she'd acted out of insecurity. It's difficult for me to integrate fully with that, but it is where I am in my journey. It is part of the current work I'm doing on myself to continue healing and deepening compassion for myself. Growth is a process. Evolution is ongoing. I'm practicing patience.

A Quick Self Check–In Guide

The world is going to try to tell you who to be, how you need to be, and what you need in order to feel good. It preys on insecure people. I cannot emphasize enough that the relationship and connection you have to your Inner Being/Higher Self trumps everything.

- Find out who you are as soon as you can and own it without needing outside approval.
    - Like what you like and do not be embarrassed or afraid to like it.
    - Find out what you stand for and do not be ashamed to speak it.
- Be secure in who you are, even the qualities that aren't your favorite (we all have qualities that aren't great).
    - Live authentically.
    - Own your thoughts, words, likes, dislikes, actions, life.
- Elevate your consciousness and live from that space as often as you can.
- Don't compare. Instead, be inspired.
    - What you're drawn to is not an accident. The people you're drawn to are not random. You see yourself in those things and people.
    - Remember what you like in someone else is a reflection of what you like in yourself. What you don't like in someone else is a reflection of what you don't like about yourself.
- Evolve. Learn and change for the better from challenges.

- Don't settle for something you don't really want. Go through uncomfortable moments to get to where you want to be. It's okay to not know what you're doing. Nobody knows what the fuck they're doing.

- Forgive.

- Release attachment to a specific outcome because what you're really seeking is a feeling.

- Take social media breaks.

- Remember to breathe.

We're all going to feel fear. We're all going to know scarcity. We're all going to feel the pressure to conform. We're all going to acknowledge doubt. We all have insecurities. We all want to feel safe. But it's where you make your decisions and live your life from that matters. We all have your mud puddles. Where are you being held back from living in your true fulfillment? Use this self check–in to shift into alignment with what is going to move you forward and help get you to where you want to be and live the life that you're truly meant to live.

You can be standing in love/trust and still feel fear. That's real. Just know that if you're standing in fear, it will be near impossible to feel the love and trust. Fear is that powerful. Referencing Elizabeth Gilbert in her book *Big Magic*, she very eloquently talks about how fear comes along with her when starting a new creative endeavor, but she puts fear in the back seat. Fear doesn't drive her actions nor does it get a say in the energy around what she's creating. She acknowledges it as a real thing but she doesn't stand in it. That is how you must treat the left side of the following exercise if you really want to move forward in living your most fulfilling life.

Are you Aligning with?

Lack or Fulfillment
Scarcity or Abundance
Fear or Love/Trust
Victim-hood or Empowerment
Conformity or Authenticity
Doubt or Certainty
Outer approval or Inner approval
Insecurity or Security
Staying in safety or Being in curiosity
Being in your head or Being in your present

It Was Never About the Boy or the Kids - Release Attachment to Outcomes

And one last thing... it turns out that it was not about the boy. Or kids. Or not kids. I used to place so much emphasis on those ideas, but it truly wasn't. If I want children and they happen for me, great! Yes, my story has a boy in it. But my boy did not save me. Trust me, at times I wanted him to, but he didn't. I did the work on myself to rebuild my foundation and he gave me a safe space to explore, vent, cry and celebrate—but he did not save me. I saved myself.

There is no right and wrong when it comes to having children or not having children. I think so many women who are unsure if they want to have children really struggle with there being one "right" way. A lot of that comes from what people say when you state that you don't want kids. "Oh, you'll change your mind," they say. What that really says is that it wouldn't be OK if you didn't change your mind. You've got to be really grounded in who you are to not let a comment like that affect you.

You are here to experience the journey of self-discovery and no two journeys are the same. They are supposed to be drastically different. As much as you might want to experience the same things for human connection (getting married, having kids and buying a home), many times you need to experience life differently in order to learn about yourself on a deeper level. We don't all need to agree that having children is the be-all and end-all label of success and a "happy ending". Not all happy endings look alike.

Instead of replying, "You'll change your mind.", let there be space. Let the people that you are speaking to have the space that they deserve to discover what is genuinely in alignment for their life.

All I know, right now, is that I'm fulfilled in my life. There may come a day when I want children. That day may come tomorrow or it may come in ten years. I'm not attached to an outcome of what that needs to look like for me. If in ten years I am not able to have my own children because I waited too long, there are millions of children who need homes and if I want children bad enough, it won't matter how they come to me. Jake and I agreed before we got married that if one of us wants children, we would do that with and for each other.

If any of you are struggling with whether or not to have children, I urge you to release that for a bit. Connect deeper with yourself and, if you find that you do want to raise a human, then release attachment as to how that needs to look and embrace that it will look the way it will look for you. Trust that. Don't be fearful.

One of my dear friends tried for years to get pregnant. She went through tremendous heartache and agonizing pain. It was shortly after she adopted her first child that she started The Adoption Hope Foundation to help break the financial barrier of adoption by providing grants to people who choose to build their families through adoption. What a beautiful gift she is giving the world. Would she have been inspired to create such a project had she been able to have her own baby? Maybe. But maybe not.

Trust in your journey. There are big things waiting to be revealed. Allow yourself to feel pain because pain changes you. It will lead you to miraculous discoveries about yourself that help you leave your fingerprint on the world. Sometimes you must be willing to let go of what you thought life was supposed to be to allow it to be what it needs to be. Release attachment to specific outcomes.

Coming Full Circle

In August of 2014, after just under a year of being back together, Jake and I headed East for a friend's wedding and our annual East Coast trip. We had decided that since we were back together, we'd make a stop in good 'ol Oneonta, NY.

We grabbed some cold cheese pizza (a college fave) and headed up to campus. They had made several updates and, I must say, our college was looking quite nice. I was hoping we'd go to the sidewalk that splits where I invited him over for a beer and he, days later, asked for my screen name. I couldn't tell which one of us was leading us there.

Once we got there, Jake set up his camera to take a photo at our special place. Or so I thought that's what he was doing. It was transition time and college kids were walking to and from class. Some were getting off the bus at the same stop that we would get off at together. We posed, though I never saw the flash. Then he turned to me and said, "Lex, we have a lot of good memories at this sidewalk and we are about to have one more."

He got down on one knee and proposed. Video rolling—no wonder I hadn't seen a flash.

Nine years after inviting him over for a bowl of Kix and his asking for my screen name in that very spot, I was getting engaged. I don't think I could've planned it better myself.

References

Baker, T. *The 1% Rule: How to Fall in Love with the Process and Achieve Your Wildest Dreams*, Scotts Valley: CreateSpace Independent Publishing Platform, 2018.

Brown, B. *Daring Greatly*, New York: Avery 2015.

Gilbert, G. *Big Magic*, New York: Riverhead Books 2016.

"The Flight of the Hummingbird, the Curiosity Driven Life," *Oprah's SuperSoul Conversations*, CC-TV 14, October 13, 2015, Television.

The Off Camera Show, *"Brit Marling of Netflix 'The OA' had a Near Death Experience at Goldman Sachs,"* posted on March 22, 2017, YouTube video, 7:22, https://www.youtube.com/watch?v=t6ZMaBAlgwM.